Hit the Job Writing

JOSEPH JUDGE

RISE AND SHINE PRESS • WAYNE, PENNSYLVANIA

Copyright 2013 by Joseph Judge.

All rights reserved. No part of this book may be used, reproduced, or transmitted in any form or by any means whatsoever—with the exception of a reviewer who may quote brief passages in a review to be printed in a newspaper or magazine—without the written permission of the publisher. For information, contact Rise and Shine Press, P.O. Box 11, Wayne, PA 19087.

Cover design by Beth Fazio

ISBN 978-0-9774099-2-1
Printed in the United States of America

Rise and Shine Press
P.O. Box 11
Wayne, PA 19087

Table of Contents

Foreword vii

Introduction ix

The cost of bad writing is larger than you think. ❖ We have too many excuses for bad writing. ❖ Improved writing comes from writing. ❖ Please scribble through this book.

Section I: Getting Started   1

1. **First Thoughts**   3

   First, consider not writing at all. ❖ Write both: subject and purpose. ❖ Envision your reader reading. ❖ Brainstorm by drawing clusters.

2. **Pen to Paper**   15

   Opening lines are important. ❖ Organize like a movie director. ❖ Outline: avoid the table of contents. ❖ Blast out a complete draft, then rest.

Section II: Making it Correct   37

3. **On Your Marks**   39

   His, hers, its: no apostrophe fits. ❖ Comma rules are really guidelines. ❖ Use marks to interrupt the reading. ❖ Use marks to join or group things.

4. **Matching Words**   55

   Verbs must match subjects: always. ❖ Pronouns must match, or: delays. ❖ Modifiers must match, or: confusion.

5. **The Right Words**   67

   Who/whom? Try using IC-WaWa. ❖ Use memory aids for homonyms. ❖ Idiom is learned by hearing it.

6. **Department of Corrections   83**

   Correctness? You be the judge. ❖ Rules, usage, opinions: your choice. ❖ Use proofreading tricks, or diligence. ❖ Practice with the 15 biggies.

Section III: Making it Effective   95

7. **In Search of Clarity   97**

   Choose clarity, or get un-chosen. ❖ Trim the unnecessary and redundant. ❖ Conflicted verbs need replacing. ❖ Align grammar to the story.

8. **Good Behavior   123**

   Find alternatives to negative words. ❖ Nix words that make you sound biased. ❖ Minimize the use of mumbo jumbo. ❖ Talk with and about your reader.

9. **Words with Impact   139**

   Every word counts. ❖ Trim, shape, and color. ❖ Say much, with few words. ❖ Use the pyramid of concise writing.

10. **Easy Reading   151**

    Active voice makes reading easy. ❖ Parallels make comprehension easy. ❖ Transitions and links guide the reader. ❖ Sentence variety keeps readers awake.

Section IV: Style & Format   173

11. **Document Style   175**

    Announce with purpose and focus. ❖ Make letters consistent and assertive. ❖ Presentation charts should be sparse. ❖ Fill your résumé with action verbs.

12. **Email Style   195**

    Always write the message first. ❖ Use contractions as your default style. ❖ Extra care can fine tune the tone. ❖ Make subject lines interesting to read.

13. **Report Style   207**

    Group ideas in a logical hierarchy. ❖ The status report: answer questions. ❖ Write summaries last, but place first. ❖ Guidelines help with writing numbers.

14. **Looking Good   229**

    Choose fonts for the whole picture. ❖ Try to avoid using justification. ❖ Blank space is a design feature: use it. ❖ Loosen, list, and layer for readability.

Section V: Finesse   245

15. **Tactful Writing   247**

    Style is how you write. ❖ Tone is what they hear. ❖ Be as direct as your position allows. ❖ Be as personal as your purpose allows.

16. **Diplomatic Writing   257**

    Respond to nastiness with control. ❖ Be the Earth: firmly address. ❖ Be the Wind: gently redirect. ❖ Be the Fire: and disappoint your mom.

17. **Persuasive Writing   267**

    Speak your reader's language. ❖ Adjust strategy to circumstances. ❖ Remember primacy and recency. ❖ Use rhythm to make an impression.

18. **Promotional Writing   279**

    Above all, do not be dull. ❖ An honest self-interview helps. ❖ Try the BrBrBp Roadmap. ❖ Choose words that compel.

Acknowledgements 293

About the Author 293

Index 295

List of Exercises 301

Resources 303

Foreword

"No one writes anymore." Really?

It is true that, much to the chagrin of many grandparents, the art of a personal, handwritten letter may soon be lost. Teachers aren't much happier when they learn that the infamous 5-paragraph SAT essay they labor to teach disinterested students is useful only for … the SATs. So we no longer write, right? Think again.

In this digital age, we actually write (should we say "type"?) more than ever. For many, email has replaced phone calls and face-to-face meetings. We rely on electronic forms of writing to communicate to people in the next cubicle or on the next continent. Status reports, meeting summaries, problem reports, operating procedures, promotional material, product descriptions, user manuals, safety instructions, research findings: these and more are still needed. In some sectors, the threat of lawsuits requires more accurate and complete records than ever before. Imagine how the world would function if all these forms of communication were written badly.

Still not convinced? Consider this: The College Board's study of 120 top American corporations concluded, "In today's workplace, writing is a 'threshold skill' for hiring and promotion among salaried employee—a ticket to professional opportunity, while poorly written job applications are a figurative kiss of death." The report also said writing skills can make the difference in a decision about who to keep and who to let go. And sadly, the study noted, "The strength of corporate complaints about the writing skills of college graduates was surprisingly powerful."

The fact is, we do write a lot at work, and our bosses are complaining that we aren't very good at it. If you want to land and keep a well-paying job, you need to be able to write well.

The mission of this workbook is to help interns and recent college graduates develop essential workplace skills so they can be successful in their chosen careers. We were thrilled when Joe Judge proposed a workbook on business writing to complement ***Hit the Job Running: Because Landing the Job is the Easy Part.*** With his unique voice, Joe makes this sometimes dry topic entertaining. He hones in on the dimensions of writing that most frequently give people problems. Recognizing that good writing comes through practice, Joe provides many opportunities to do so. Devote yourself to working through these pages and you will be delighted to see…results. Results from your writing, and consequently in your career advancement.

Continued success to you!

Andrea Dolph & Linda Dowd

Introduction

Consider this text from a government report:

> Recording illnesses has historically been a problem for employers, especially chronic or long term latent illnesses. This table is furnished to assist employers in making accurate illness determinations.

As we read it, our mind bothers us with odd questions: Is *recording* a verb or an adjective? Isn't *historically* redundant? Chronic employers? What is a *term illness*? Are companies actually allowed to find out about latent illnesses? What else is the table furnished with, silverware? Are employees determined to be ill? Why did the emphasis change from recording to determining? Is this really about observing, or is it about judging?

You don't have to look far to find examples of bad writing at work. We should recognize, however, that the problem is not limited to government. Surveys of employers conclude, with more conviction every year, that most of their employees need better writing skills.

What is the cost of bad writing? "Ten percent of sales!"

Seriously, many executives give this round number from their real-world experience. And that only estimates lost opportunities; it does not include losses in productivity.

Consider the software industry and a product that is released with poorly written documentation. Here are just some of the problems that lead to increased costs:

- Increase in product returns.
- Increase in calls to the service center.
- Decrease in repeat business as customers get irritated.
- Decrease in credibility as angry customers complain to friends.

See if you can guess the answer to the following question.

Question: What are the most common excuses for tolerating bad writing at work?

(A) Public education should have taught them enough English.

(B) We bought computers, so they should be helping.

(C) It's too difficult to assess the cost of bad writing.

(D) Writing well is hard work and time consuming.

(E) All of the above.

Unfortunately, the answer is (E). We are all part of the problem: we tolerate it every day. We should cut that out.

So what? Not my problem? Think again. Please. You worked hard in school, so you should know that with any skill there's always room for improvement. And effective writing isn't just another skill. It's a crucial skill for your success at work.

You can develop that skill by reading books on writing, but you will only learn so much. Real progress comes from real practice. This book is not just a textbook; it's a workbook, full of exercises for you to try, with solutions to consider once you're done giving it a try. Please do. Get out a pencil and scribble all over these pages. It's the best way to learn this material.

SECTION I

Getting Started

For many people, writing is a chore, and writing at work is assumed to be nothing but pain. The main reason we adopt this distressing state of mind is that we have too often experienced the agony of re-writing stuff we thought we had done well enough on the first try. The key to avoiding major re-writing is up-front thinking and planning. Easy, now. Relax. It'll all be over before you know it. Your reward will, unfortunately, not be a lollipop. It'll be kudos from colleagues for a job well done.

Chapter 1: First Thoughts – Before we write, we think. How well we think, and how well that thinking contributes to good writing, is the result of effort and technique. It's going to be your effort. The first chapter will provide the techniques you can use to take advantage of all that impressive thinking you will be doing.

Chapter 2: Pen to Paper – Before we write, we should plan. You're cringing, right? Sounds like drudgery? Okay, fair enough. But it is important, as will be explained. With a little of your effort and a few simple techniques, you can start your writing with the confidence of someone backed up by a team of deep-thinking, thorough-planning English majors dedicated to your success.

~ Subject in Action ~

Liz and Helen met in orientation on their first day of work. They became close friends, seeing each other not just in the office but socializing after hours. For the most part, they were friends, not competitors. But there was one thing about Helen that increasingly made Liz jealous: When Helen had to write any kind of report or presentation, she could sit down and type up a crystal-clear piece of writing in what seemed like no time at all. Liz, on the other hand, labored over her documents for days – writing and re-writing.

One day Liz told Helen how envious she was that Helen could sit down and effortlessly write with such clarity and speed. Helen told Liz she was wrong. What Liz couldn't see was that Helen spent a lot of time thinking about what she was going to write and scribbling down the ideas along the way. She thought about what outcome she wanted from the writing, what her message needed to be, who needed to read it, what they needed to know (and not know), and the best flow of the information. She jotted down ideas, phrases, drawings: linked them, ranked them, and crossed some of them out. But after typing out her first draft, she threw away her scratch paper, so Liz didn't see the evidence of all that work. "The stuff I throw away," Helen said, "is my version of one of those big boards you see on police detective shows, full of notes and photos and links and questions. It's a big honking scrapbook I can stand back and look at."

Helen saved a lot of time in re-writes. She may have put as much time in as Liz, but much of the work went on in her mind as it poured out into scribbles early on. Because of this, her first drafts were ready to go before she even started typing. Writing was a release, not a frustration. Liz gave it a try. At first she wasn't very good at it, but eventually she, too, could write with Helen's seeming ease.

CHAPTER 1

First Thoughts

> **In This Chapter**
>
> - First, consider not writing at all.
> - Write both: subject and purpose.
> - Envision your reader reading.
> - Brainstorm by drawing clusters.

WHY YOU SHOULD CARE

This will happen (sorry): you write a document, edit it, perfect it, and submit it; your boss reads it, frowns, and says, "What were you thinking?" This is not a critique of your writing skills; it's a complaint about how little thinking you did before you started writing. Try not to do that too often. Try instead to start your writing by not writing right away: sit back, take a deep breath, and think carefully about what you need to *accomplish*, not about what you think you need to write. The result will be better writing from the beginning and a boss who is impressed by your willingness to be careful.

DECIDE

In the space below, take two minutes to write a brief email:

1. A description of a recent frustrating event at work.
2. What you would like to see done about it.

Subject: Frustration and Solution

_____

_____

_____

_____

_____

Now, for each of the questions below, select an answer:

	Yes	Maybe	No
Have I a good reason for writing this? (I might be venting or trying to impress.)			
Am I the right person to write this? (They might prefer to hear from another.)			
Is this the right time to be writing it? (It might be too tense at work now.)			
Should I really put it in writing? (Once I write it, I can't ever take it back.)			
Is this preferred to verbal delivery? (Their reaction might change what I say.)			

Based on these answers, should you seriously consider perfecting and sending your email? If you did not check off the entire Yes column, you have reason to stop right there. If you said Yes to everything, but had a nagging voice inside you saying, "well, maybe that one is a Maybe," then you have good reason to pause.

DEFINE

Many people believe that writing is an act of improvisation. This mistaken belief contributes to procrastination and lazy thinking. It is the first step on the path to bad writing. The first step on the other path, the one to good writing, starts with a simple exercise in planning: writing down the subject *and* the purpose. Choose something you wrote recently: an email, a letter, or a report. Write down the subject and the purpose:

Subject:

_____

Purpose:

_____

Consider new guidelines for writing a subject and a purpose:

Subject: Use five words or fewer, but do not use any verbs or verb-like constructions.

Purpose: Write one brief sentence. Begin with one of the four verbs below, identify the reader, and include an instance of a suitable topic:

verb	↔	reader	↔	topic
inform	↔	Bob	↔	facts
instruct	↔	Bob	↔	tasks
motivate	↔	Bob	↔	behaviors
persuade	↔	Bob	↔	decisions

Consider this example:

First scribbles:

Subject: All employees must begin the workday at 9 AM

Purpose: Complain about Bob being late to work all the time.

(unclear)

Second try:

Subject: Tardiness

Purpose: Motivate Bob to show up on time.

(concise & clear)

Now take the second step on the path to good writing. Be more concise and clear by rewriting your original subject and purpose according to the new guidelines:

New Subject: (use no verbs)

_____

New Purpose: (use verb and topic)

_____

Okay, it's time to sit back and think. Would you have written the document differently? This simple but powerful writing habit is useful for several reasons:

- It promotes early scribbling to generate ideas.
- It separates subject from purpose to encourage clear thinking, which leads to clear writing.

DESCRIBE

When was the last time you stopped yourself from writing something so that you could first think about your reader?

"Gosh! I forgot to do a thorough analysis of my reader. I just can't write well without doing that first."

Uh huh, thought so. Assessing the reader is like flossing: we know it's beneficial, but we don't do it as often as we should. Teachers told us to do it, but they seldom forced us to try it. Well, here is your chance to actually give it a try. Don't worry, it will all be over before you know it.

The task is this:

- Visualize your reader in the act of reading what you have written.

Okay, so how do we *visualize*? The key to getting the most benefit from the least amount of effort is to use the technique that is best suited to you. Some people work best with words; others work best with images.

Let's first try a word-oriented approach:

- For the most recent significant thing you wrote at work, identify the reader and fill in a brief response about that reader for each topic or question in the table on the next page.

Be brief, be candid, and maybe just have fun.

Who:
Their job title and level of education.
Their attitude towards me.
What:
What do they know about it?
What should they do after reading it?
Where:
Where will they read it?
Where are they in the hierarchy?
Why:
Why will they read it?
Why would they react to it?
When:
When will they read it?
When will they react to it?
How:
How interested are they in it?
How will they be affected by it?

Now ask yourself: Would this activity guide me to write in a way that makes it easier for the reader to get my message? If you answered, "No," you may be fooling yourself. There is always room for improvement.

DEPICT

The other way to visualize your reader is to do it visually, using pictures. One approach is presented here, using stick people. Yes, that's right, stick people. The sillier the memory aid, the more effective it can be. Have fun drawing something for each of the items in the diagram below.

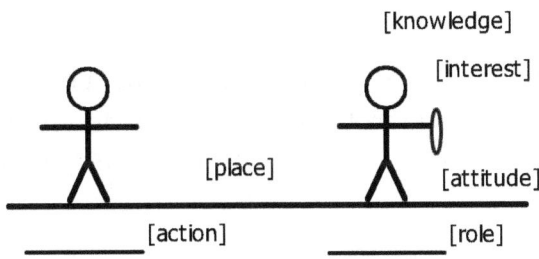

item	description	possibilities
action	What you want to do.	inform, advise, persuade
role	The role of the reader.	colleague, boss, customer
place	Where it will be read.	office, hotel, home
knowledge	What the reader knows about the subject.	big brain: expert small brain: uninformed
interest	How interested the reader is with the subject.	big ear: very interested small ear: indifferent
attitude	How the reader feels about you.	flowers: likes you cigar: indifferent dagger: out to get you

Here is an example:

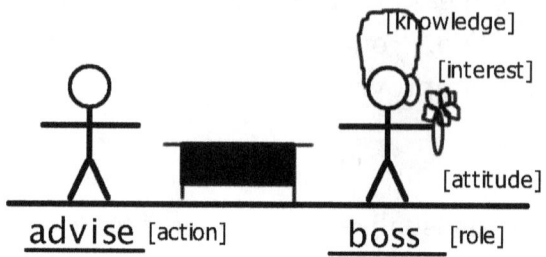

You are writing to advise your boss. Your boss will read it at work (the desk). Your boss has extensive knowledge about the subject (big brain), is interested (respectable-sized ear), and thinks well of you (flowers).

Now it's your turn. Use the diagram below. For a recent significant thing you wrote at work, write down two words, for the action and the role, and then draw fanciful images for the other items.

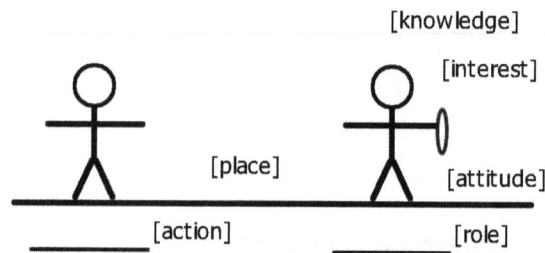

Again, ask yourself: Would this activity guide me to write in a way that makes it easier for the reader to get my message?

Use your own pictures if you are image-oriented. Use your own list of questions if you are word-oriented. But, for the sake of your reader, visualize your reader reading your work. It's doodling worth doing for any writing that's important to your success.

BRAINSTORM

Think back to when you received the offer for your current job. Now pretend you are writing an email accepting the job offer. Take a minute to think about it. Better yet, take three minutes, 180 seconds exactly, to play "word association" and to continue filling out the diagram below. Let your brain wander; make a new circle for each connecting thought that arises.

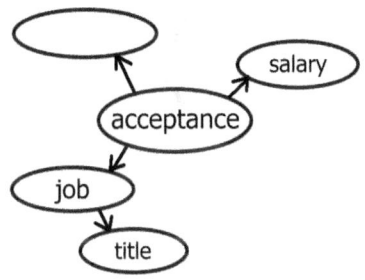

Reflection

At what point in time did you feel like saying, "Okay, now I know what I want to write, so can I stop doing this?" Typically, this happens at about two minutes. How many circles are in your diagram? If there are fewer than ten you were not having enough fun.

This type of free association, sometimes called clustering or mind mapping, uses both sides of your brain: right for insight, left for logic. It also uses both levels of your psyche: unconscious for creating, conscious for refining.

When you draw a cluster, you map an interior landscape as your ideas emerge. It is effective because it reflects the way your creative mind works with thoughts and images: it groups things and it jumps, seemingly randomly, between groups.

If you have trouble with clustering, it is most likely due to your conscious mind trying to stay in control. If this happens, just doodle by drawing connected circles, with nothing inside them. As you relax and continue, your conscious mind will step aside.

Goal 1

When mind-mapping with clusters, the goal is not just the quantity of circles and quality of topics in the circles. More importantly, the goal is to identify things that you might otherwise have missed.

Goal 2

For some writers, the goal is to jumpstart the writing process.

FINAL COMMENTS

Those who pause and think carefully before placing their fingers over a keyboard will never know how badly they might have messed up. That's a good thing: they avoid the road not taken, the road to inefficient work habits and rambling writing that has to be totally revamped.

Every exercise in this chapter asked you to take a pencil and write something on the page. This has a purpose: to convince you that this is an extremely valuable habit. How much paper do you throw away at work? Try this: keep it for a while, turn it over, write down thoughts, scribble diagrams. You can always throw it away. No one will see what you wrote. But everyone will notice how your writing gets better and clearer as you scribble and doodle.

FAQs

Q: *I know my subject. I know my purpose. Why spend time writing them down?*

A: Two reasons: (1) You often need to adapt or change them to new things learned as you write down your first draft and then edit. Things committed to memory are not easily changed. Things committed to paper are changed with a few pencil scribbles. (2) You should leave yourself open to the possibility that what you know now isn't perfect. The act of writing it down can bring surprising new ideas and clarity of description.

Q: *I'm new in my job so I don't really know my readers very well. How can I analyze my readers if I don't know them?*

A: You make assumptions and imagine them. Ideally, imagine just one—the most important one, the person who could make the most important decision based on what you wrote. Sound flakey? Yeah, okay, it might feel that way the first couple of times. But give it a try. Don't overdo it with elaborate details and diagrams. This is a brief effort: jotting down and doodling.

Q: *Often when I write at work, I have many readers of the same email or document. What should I do if the readers know different things or have different priorities?*

A: Practice choosing the most important reader. When writing for that reader, practice not offending or boring the second most important reader. Tricky stuff, this. Welcome to the working world. It can get awfully complicated awfully fast. But you'll get there. Actually, you're already ahead of the game: you're reading this and giving it serious thought.

Q: *In my job, I don't have to write very often so when I do, it's very difficult for me. Any suggestions for how to make it easier?*

A: Suggestion #1 – Practice in a low-stress environment: this book. Suggestion #2 – Ask yourself: Do I want my coworkers to fail at what they do? (Be nice.) No, you don't. And no, they don't want you to fail. They want you to do well, and they will give you a break if you write something that isn't worthy of *Atlantic Monthly*. They will always cut you some slack, especially if with each effort you learn a little and you improve a little.

CHAPTER 2

Pen to Paper

In This Chapter

- Opening lines are important.
- Organize like a movie director.
- Outline: avoid the table of contents.
- Blast out a complete draft, then rest.

WHY YOU SHOULD CARE

This will also happen (sorry, again): you think carefully, then write and submit a document; your boss reads it, frowns, and says, "Why did you write it that way?" This is a complaint that you didn't do a good job of organizing what it was you had to say. When this happens you will be viewed as someone who doesn't care about the quality of your work.

The solution is simple: a bit of planning, a little organizing, and some outlining. There it is, the dreaded word: outline. Shame on your school teachers for making it such dreaded work. It's time to get past the distasteful memories and learn a new way to use outlines that is both painless and surprisingly helpful.

OPEN

The opening lines of things we write at work are extremely important. A good opening ensures that our writing will be read instead of discarded. And it gives the reader a mental road map early in their journey through our document.

How not to write it: Far too often, we write openings after assuming one of the following fallacies:
- Any opening will do; I can wing it.
- Everything I have to say is so useful, anything can go first.
- Readers should experience it in the same sequence I did.
- To convince people, I must order things as I would in a mathematical proof.
- To appear most professional, I should use the format of an academic research paper.
- To avoid initial negative reactions, I should delay controversial findings until the end.

How to write it: The best techniques are the simplest:
- Write it early, expecting to modify it repeatedly.
- Write it as a separate thing, just as you wrote the purpose.
- Write it as a brief paragraph; expand it later if needed.
- Consider it the verbal description you would give to the reader, who unexpectedly meets you in an elevator and asks what you are writing but has only a few moments.

What it should say: The opening of every document should include three components:

Issues – Explain what it is you are writing about.

Details – Preview the main ideas you are presenting.

Findings – Introduce conclusions or recommendations.

Exercises

The following opening will not help the reader much. Which fallacy does it use?

To decide whether to switch HMOs, a request was made for an independent review of your health plan. The HR department selected the author to interview employees and contact alternative HMOs. Access to HMOs proceeded smoothly; they were very receptive and eager to negotiate favorable terms. It was only after these efforts that the author was able to interview employees; it took that long for the HR department to get buy-in from annoyed supervisors. After organizing data and analyzing alternatives, the author prepared this report and submits it for management review.

fallacy: _____

Here is an opening that does help the reader, but it's missing a component. Which one?

The purpose of this announcement is to recommend a new dental plan provider. We investigated who could provide adequate coverage at reasonable costs. There were difficulties finding a plan that met all our needs, but we succeeded.

component: _____

Rewrite the opening to the Declaration of Independence:

When in the Course of human events, it becomes necessary for one people to dissolve the political bands which have connected them with another, and to assume among the powers of the earth, the separate and equal station to which the Laws of Nature and of Nature's God entitle them, a decent respect to the opinions of mankind requires that they should declare the causes which impel them to the separation.

Use one brief sentence for each of the three components (issues, details, findings) and put them in any suitable order. Don't worry about how Thomas Jefferson wrote it; write your own clear and assertive version.

Solutions

fallacy:

3. Readers should experience it in the same sequence I did.

component: findings   (which provider?)

This document declares our independence. (findings)
We felt it necessary to give the reasons for our decision. (issues)
Our many grievances against the tyrant are listed below. (details)

With this solution we are suggesting that the order of the components is not as important as the presence of all three components. Whether this replacement opening is good, or whether yours is good, is obviously a subjective issue.

ORGANIZE

Early in the writing process, it can help if you pretend to be a diplomat and a director.

Diplomat

Organize your writing to be tactful. The effort you put into preparing your reader for your main point should vary directly with how much you think your point will make life difficult for your reader. As part of this effort, consider these general rules of diplomacy:

- When asking for something, give reasons before requests.
    - Your opening will alert the reader to the nature of the request.
    - State your reasons with as much detail as you think your readers are willing to read.
- When the topic is contentious, give details before conclusions.
    - Giving details first at least gives you a chance to educate them.
    - Giving conclusions early will only turn off those you really need to convince.
- When giving a refusal, explain before you refuse.
    - This is most appropriate when the explanation is brief and you want to maintain future goodwill.
    - Open with a neutral statement, give the explanation, give the refusal clearly, and end on a positive note.

Director

Organize your document so that readers will be so engaged that they can't put it down. A useful analogy is that your document is a movie and you are the director, implementing the activities below.

activities		director's view:
List:	topics	character events
Sort:	topics into groups	events into scenes
Order:	groups in logical sequence	scenes into a movie

The third step, ordering, is the one most often neglected by people in their writing at work. But it is the most important step for engaging the reader, who prefers carefully sequenced ideas in a document (or scenes in a movie).

Example: Assume the opening below will be used. Sort each topic in the list by putting it in group A, B, or C, which have been given brief titles. Then, be a diplomat and a director: order the groups.

Opening: Maintenance of our website grew in difficulty, so we request that you increase our budget.

1	design of new website section $32,000 to outsource	→ ☐
2	peaks in website traffic jam the network	→ ☐
3	$45,000 for additional webmaster	→ ☐
4	one major update to a website section each month	→ ☐
5	$15,000 for artwork and proofreading	→ ☐
6	ten updated webpages promoted daily	→ ☐
7	publications department is always growing	→ ☐
8	webmaster spends less time on intranet design	→ ☐
9	upgrade our network connection: $6,000	→ ☐
10	new sales division demands more assistance	→ ☐
11	network engineer monitors and reports on traffic	→ ☐
12	webmaster coordinates content development	→ ☐

A: requested budget increases Order: ☐ → ☐ → ☐
B: maintenance activities
C: maintenance difficulties

Solution:

1	design of new website section $32,000 to outsource	→	A
2	peaks in website traffic jam the network	→	C
3	$45,000 for additional webmaster	→	A
4	one major update to a website section each month	→	B
5	$15,000 for artwork and proofreading	→	A
6	ten updated webpages promoted daily	→	B
7	publications department is always growing	→	C
8	webmaster spends less time on intranet design	→	C
9	upgrade our network connection: $6,000	→	A
10	new sales division demands more assistance	→	C
11	network engineer monitors and reports on traffic	→	B
12	webmaster coordinates content development	→	B

A: requested budget increases
B: maintenance activities
C: maintenance difficulties

Order: B → C → A

(When asking for something, give reasons before requests.)

Exercise

Assume the opening below will be used. Sort each topic by putting it in group A, B, or C, which have been given brief titles. Then, be a diplomat and a director: order the groups.

Opening: Analysis of our controversial transition to all online training shows that we still need classroom training.

1	users of online courses show low completion rates	
2	training effectiveness has degraded	
3	managers are too busy to use online courses	
4	classroom training had better test scores	
5	the main training users are now less committed to training	
6	managers were the dominant users of classroom training	
7	outside trainers are reluctant to convert to online format	
8	our relations with outside trainers is suffering	
9	half of classroom courses were designed by outside trainers	

A: online training
B: training conclusions
C: classroom training

Order: ☐ → ☐ → ☐

Solution

1	users of online courses show low completion rates	A
2	training effectiveness has degraded	B
3	managers are too busy to use online courses	A
4	classroom training had better test scores	C
5	the main training users are now less committed to training	B
6	managers were the dominant users of classroom training	C
7	outside trainers are reluctant to convert to online format	A
8	our relations with outside trainers is suffering	B
9	half of classroom courses were designed by outside trainers	C

A: online training
B: training conclusions
C: classroom training

Order: A → C → B

or:

C → A → B

(When the topic is contentious, give details before conclusions.)

OUTLINE

Outlines grow up to be first drafts. This can be a good thing: it can keep you from wandering or getting stuck while writing your first draft. But it can also be a bad thing: flaws in the outline are typically preserved in the first draft. Four pieces of advice will help:

Use a successful model.

> It's natural and efficient to base your outline on a company template or a copy of someone else's document.

Use veto power.

> If the subject and purpose aren't fully supported by the format of the company template, give veto power to your subject and purpose. The template is only a guide; don't let it bully you.

Avoid one-word headings.

> When you are outlining, you should be generating possibilities, not summarizing. One-word headings restrict thought and look more like stop signs than green lights when you use the outline to write your first draft. Use brief statements for all headings in your outline. If company policy requires one-word headings, add them later.

Avoid the table of contents.

> Your writing plan starts to freeze when you use numbers and letters. Keep your outline flexible: use bullets and dashes.

Exercise

For the outline below, assume the subject and purpose are accurate. Let's make these changes:
- Delete irrelevant sections.
- Replace one-word headings with brief instructive sentences.
- Make it look less like a table of contents.

Subject: Computer virus security procedures

Purpose: Instruct employees to avoid and kill viruses.

Outline: (draft)

    I. History of the computer virus
       A. 1982 to 1998
       B. Recent IT woes
    II. Consequences of a virus
       A. Productivity
       B. Intellectual property
       C. Reputation
    III. Protect against a virus
       A. Employees
          1. Use a virus-scanning program
          2. Block executable code
          3. Make regular backups
       B. Departments
          1. Distribute security announcements
          2. Audit anti-virus software
    IV. Follow emergency procedures
       A. Isolate your computer
       B. Call the hotline

Solution

Subject: Computer virus security procedures

Purpose: Instruct employees to avoid and kill viruses.

Outline: (still a draft, just a better draft)

- Protect against a virus
    - **Employees should take responsibility**
        - Use a virus-scanning program
        - Block executable code
        - Make regular backups
    - **Departments should educate and audit**
        - Distribute security announcements
        - Audit anti-virus software
- Follow emergency procedures
    - Isolate your computer
    - Call the hotline

(Irrelevant sections: I, II)

Exercise

For the outline below, assume the subject and purpose are accurate. Make these changes:

- Delete the unnecessary section.
- Make it look less like a table of contents.
- Replace one-word headings with brief assertive sentences.

Subject: _A multicultural organization_
Purpose: _Instruct leaders to address diversity._

1. Leadership
    1.1 Make diversity a core value.
    1.2 Include managing diversity in our strategy.
    1.3 Commit resources for the long-term.
2. Education
    2.1 Give workshops about diversity issues.
    2.2 Provide introductory as well as advanced training.
    2.3 Develop in-house training expertise.
3. Measurement
    3.1 Assess equal-opportunity profile data.
    3.2 Survey attitudes and perceptions of employees.
    3.3 Track differential career experiences.
4. Culture
    4.1 Definitions suffer from semantic confusion.
    4.2 Views include integration, differentiation, and fragmentation.
    4.3 Researchers identify norms, values, rules, and myths.

Solution

Subject: <u>A multicultural organization</u>
Purpose: <u>Instruct leaders to address diversity.</u>

- **Address diversity at the highest level.**
    - → Make diversity a core value.
    - → Include managing diversity in our strategy.
    - → Commit resources for the long-term.
- **Train employees to value diversity.**
    - → Give workshops about diversity issues.
    - → Provide introductory as well as advanced training.
    - → Develop in-house training expertise.
- **Collect information about diversity issues.**
    - → Assess equal-opportunity profile data.
    - → Survey attitudes and perceptions of employees.
    - → Track differential career experiences.

unnecessary section: 4

DRAFT

Think about the most recent example of an important thing you wrote at work. For each of the four questions below, mark a spot on the line to give your best subjective answer.

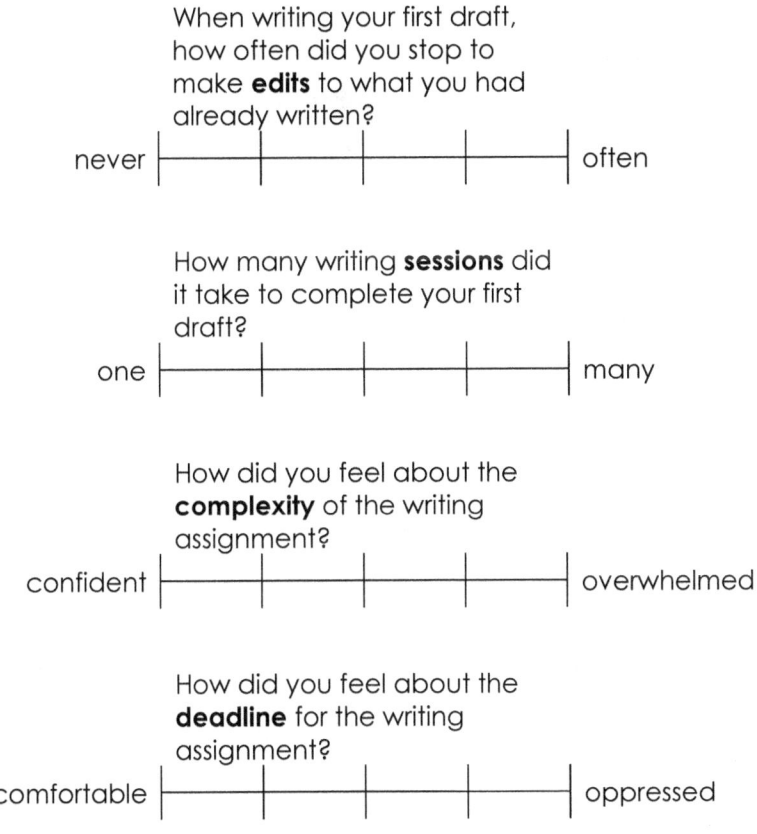

Admittedly, some of these things are out of your control. Your employer typically controls deadlines, and your boss often controls complexity. You have some control over sessions and usually total control over edits. The ideal spot on all four lines is the far left. Surprised? Keep reading.

The optimal way to write a first draft is this: *quickly write it all down before you change any of it.* The reasons are as follows:

1. **You will finish faster.** The draft/edit/edit way of writing is much faster than the write/edit/write/edit way of writing. This helps you schedule better to meet deadlines.
2. **You will feel better.** After completing the first draft, you have a "whole document" view. This helps you assess how difficult it will be to write all later versions of the document. This reduces anxiety about complexity.
3. **You will edit better.** People who write/edit/write/edit tend to consider the early sections of the document completed, and therefore do a lazier job of editing in the final draft. Also, we edit better when we are more relaxed, which is the case when we have completed a full first draft.

How to do it

- **Be directed but flexible.** Know where you are going by using an outline as a guide. Treat your outline as you would a map when on vacation: follow logical paths, but allow brief detours.
- **Be willing to write a first draft that has holes in it.** When you come to a spot where you are missing something (idea, data, graphic, quote), skip several lines and leave a note to yourself about what is to be inserted at this spot. Then skip a few more lines and continue immediately.

Above all, remember: the first draft *should* be a mess. If you write it without using an outline, it is likely to be a useless mess. If you write it using a good outline, it will be a useful mess.

Chapter 2 ~ Pen to Paper   31

REST

It was a dark and stormy night. I was writing like there was no tomorrow. Suddenly, a voice rang out, "Please step away from the writing!" We all need a writing cop—someone who tells us to stop once in a while. "Go home! Sleep it off. Try again tomorrow." There are good reasons to be our own writing cop:

- If we refuse to stop, we can get too close to the material and lose perspective.

- When we stop writing things down, our unconscious mind has an easier time of continuing the writing and generating creative solutions to our writing problems.

In our dreams and daydreams, we recast our life incident by incident, into a form that pleases us. This reconstruction is often seeded by the conscious mind, by what is foremost on our mind. And, like it or not, our work and our writing at work are often the things that are foremost on our minds. We might as well take advantage of this by giving our unconscious mind the time to give us some valuable off-line thinking for free.

When should we do this? Actually, it happens by itself. Many writers and inventors have received their most creative insights when they were least expecting them, often while dreaming. In the examples below, draw a line to match each famous creator with the creation he dreamed.

creator	(dreamed)		creation
Samuel Coleridge, 1797	1	A	Periodic table.
Dimitri Mendeleyev, 1868	2	B	Song *Yesterday*.
Nikola Tesla, 1882	3	C	Manufacture of insulin.
Frederick Banting, 1920	4	D	Poem *Kublai Kan*.
Paul McCartney, 1965	5	E	Induction motor.
Patrick Brown, 1992	6	F	Gene chip.

Advertising guru James Webb Young said it well:

> "Out of nowhere the idea will appear. It will come when you are least expecting it—while shaving, or bathing, or most often when you are half awake in the morning."

Can you remember having a similar experience? This kind of sudden insight seldom arrives when you are trying to make it show up. Why not take advantage of this phenomenon by accepting rest as a natural part of your writing process?

Some writers find it helpful to give hints to their unconscious. You can, too. Before you go to sleep, ask yourself for help:

> "Tonight, let's come up with a creative solution to that report I'm having trouble writing."

Give it a try; it only takes a few seconds. Say it but then forget about it. Let the unconscious mind do its thing.

Solution

1-D, 2-A, 3-E, 4-C, 5-B, 6-F

FINAL COMMENTS

It kind of hurts, doesn't it? Writing down outlines that are flexible, arranging your content like a movie director, crafting opening lines that engage and inform, and pounding out that first draft that never seems to end. And all the while juggling possibilities and assessing the adequacy of all this stuff that doesn't seem to lead to anything tangible or productive. The bad news is, yeah, it's necessary to produce good writing. The good news is it gets easier every time you push yourself through it. A little pain, a lot of gain.

FAQs

Q: *What do I do when I know the reader is not going to be happy with what I have to say?*

A: When you suspect or know that the gist of your document will not be what your reader wants to hear, you should use extra care in being tactful with your opening. Here are some phrases that can help:

- The findings are surprising.
- The problem is not X, as many people thought, but Y.
- The conclusion, which no one would have predicted given previous experience, is Z.

Q: *Planning what I'm going to write takes so much time. Is all this effort really necessary?*

A: I'm going to answer two questions: Is planning necessary? Why does it have to take so much time?

First, yes, planning is necessary. Consider an analogy from the kitchen. Writing without planning is like cooking without a recipe. It works if everything is always the same. If you had to cook exquisite meals for important people, and every meal was different, would you really want to wing it every time? Creating a plan and learning to follow it is a recipe for success.

Second, it will not take more time: it will take less time. After you try it several times, you will find that you are taking less total time to complete your writing. You will also find that the work will be easier and the result will be better. You owe it to yourself to give it a try.

Q: *How do I write a strong opening sentence if I am covering many topics in one document? Should I write a paragraph of opening sentences to cover each topic? Or should I write a general sentence that might not be very informative?*

A: Write your opening sentence to shout out your response to your main goal—communicating to your most important reader that you have solved a problem and are now going to inform, or direct, or persuade the reader. And don't give me that, "Yeah, but all my topics are main goals and I have a bunch of important readers." If that's true you shouldn't be diluting all your hard work by stuffing it all in a single document. Also, almost all the time there really is only one main goal. If someone held your favorite pet over a cliff and said, "State the one and only goal, or the pet gets it," you would quickly resolve your topic conundrum. Sorry about the imagery.

Q: *I really dislike outlines. In school, I always resented when teachers made us write them. I don't see the value of them. I can organize my ideas in my head, so why bother?*

A: Many people resent outlines because teachers used them as busywork: "Outline the chapter on fiefdoms in the middle ages." Yuck. That was summarizing masquerading as outlining. Whatever way you arrived at your distaste for the act of writing outlines, you should understand that organizing ideas in your head *is* outlining. If every idea you have is perfect and every sequence of ideas you mentally arrange is perfect, ignore the advice about outlines. If you have yet to achieve perfection, writing things down can only help. Maybe try this: don't consider it outlining—call it jotting down the ideas in your head.

Q: *When I write, shouldn't I tell my reader everything I know about the subject? Isn't it the reader's job to decide what's relevant?*

A: No, and absolutely not. If the answers were yes and yes we would spend our work days turning to our coworkers and saying, "Go to Wikipedia. Figure it out." Your job is to figure something out and recommend what to do. Don't ask what your coworkers can do for themselves, ask what you can do for them.

Q: *I like to write opening sentences that are really dramatic and attention getting. Isn't it more important to get the reader's attention than to inform them of what they're about to read?*

A: In a novel, sure. In a progress report, no way—it would be merely distracting. You don't want to become the person in the office who writes as if she would rather be on Broadway. Grabbing attention is a good thing. But overshadowing the goal is not.

SECTION II

__Making it Correct__

Before putting much effort into making your writing good, make sure it's correct. Busy people at work are understandably bothered by having to stop to figure out what we mean, all because we made a simple mistake in punctuation, grammar, or vocabulary. Save their time by spending some of your time making your writing correct.

Chapter 3: On Your Marks – The apostrophe, the comma, and all the others: they exist for very good reasons. Not worrying about using them correctly leads to others not worrying about taking us seriously.

Chapter 4: Matching Words – Things that don't align cause confusion. Verbs must match with subjects. Pronouns must match with their nouns. Modifiers must clearly match the stuff they modify.

Chapter 5: The Right Words – The focus here is on the tricky things we most often get wrong: who/whom, homonyms, and idioms. For each tricky thing, there's a tricky technique to use.

Chapter 6: Department of Corrections – After you've written everything down, the real work begins: correcting the mistakes that inevitably find their way into our first drafts. We edit. We proofread. We use any trick in the book to spot and fix errors.

~ Subject in Action ~

Liam was an ambitious new hire, perhaps overly eager to quickly climb the corporate ladder and overly confident of his abilities to do so. After six months on the job, Liam was frustrated that he had not yet been promoted. It seemed to him that company leaders didn't recognize his skills and potential.

Liam decided to skip his management chain and take his problem directly to the company president. He wrote the president a long email complaining about his situation and asking for a meeting to discuss his career advancement.

When the company president read the email, it wasn't the message that irritated him the most. It was the abysmal quality of the writing. The email was full of misspellings, grammatical errors, and incorrect punctuation. The president printed the email, got out his red pen, and circled every mistake. He sent it back to Liam with the following message written at the bottom: "When you can express yourself correctly, I will be able to hear your message."

CHAPTER 3

On Your Marks

> **In This Chapter**
>
> - His, hers, its: no apostrophe fits.
> - Comma rules are really guidelines.
> - Use marks to interrupt the reading.
> - Use marks to join or group things.

WHY YOU SHOULD CARE

Simply put, you don't want to look stupid at work. Right? Picture your writing with no punctuation at all. Now picture it with wrong punctuation randomly thrown about. Both are equally useless to your reader. Both would make you look, well, not so smart. That, of course, would be a bad thing. All our punctuation should be correct. There's no excuse for mistakes with what we learned in primary school.

Beyond correctness, there is rightness. We use punctuation marks to guide the reading along, to pause the reading for something important, to assist the reading by emphasizing which things are grouped with other things. But when a mark causes the reader to stop, however briefly, and try to figure out what the heck is going on, we blew it. Try not to do that.

APOSTROPHES

Apostrophes are used for three main reasons:

Signal contractions: I'd do it, but he won't.

Show possession: Diane's company's profits are up.

Form plurals: At college in the 1990s, she got all A's.

But we will concentrate on the one use of the apostrophe that many people get wrong. The sentence below needs an apostrophe.

Its an odd parrot that mimics its own voice.

Where does it go? Should it signal a contraction? (short for *it is*) Or should it show possession? (belongs to *it*)

Apostrophes are not used with the possessive forms of personal pronouns: *his, hers, its, yours, ours, theirs*. The possessive case is already built into the word. This is not the case for impersonal pronouns: *one's, nobody's, anybody else's*. The main problem with this is the frequency with which we use the constructions *its* and *it's*. Many people either toss a coin to pick one, or just always use *it's*, settling for being correct half the time. It's not necessary—there is a solution. The key to always getting it right is to find a memory aid that works for you. Try one of these:

His, hers, its (no apostrophe fits).	Possessive personal pronouns do not use the apostrophe.
The *s* belongs to the *t*.	Show possession: make the *s* belong to the *t*, with nothing in between.

Exercises

Find and fix the problems with apostrophes:

1. Its an odd parrot that mimics its own voice.

2. It's an odd font that bends it's descenders, so mind your p's and q's.

3. Send the copier to Bob's Divisions clerks, but ask if its okay to re-use its box.

4. If its time to submit the report, it's time to dot the is and cross the ts.

5. We shouldnt pay for its shipping and handling.

6. At ten o'clock shes going to discuss the report and it's conclusions.

7. Ross's opinion was that its only the two agencies' rules that apply.
   [Note: To show possession, only add an *s* if it matches common pronunciation.]

8. Its Camerons intention that well call if we cant make it.

9. It's unfortunate our textbooks haven't arrived.

10. Its claim to fame was that it's product's sales werent falling.

Solutions

1. **It's** an odd parrot that mimics its own voice.

2. It's an odd font that bends **its** descenders, so mind your p's and q's.

3. Send the copier to Bob's **Division's** clerks, but ask if **it's** okay to re-use its box.

4. If **it's** time to submit the report, it's time to dot the **i's** and cross the **t's**.

5. We **shouldn't** pay for its shipping and handling.

6. At ten o'clock **she's** going to discuss the report and **its** conclusions.

7. Ross's opinion was that **it's** only the two agencies' rules that apply.

8. **It's Cameron's** intention that **we'll** call if we **can't** make it.

9. It's unfortunate our textbooks haven't arrived.   **[correct as is]**

10. Its claim to fame was that **its** product's sales **weren't** falling.

Rebuttals and Such

Careless New Hire: "What's the big deal, anyway? Who cares whether it's its or it's?"

Boss: "I see …"

Try not to say this sort of thing out loud. It can make you look like the young man on the sitcom, *Two And A Half Men*, whose approach to everything other than himself can be summed up in the response, "Whatever." Think about that. Would *you* hire him?

Analytical New Hire: "Emailing and messaging have created an abbreviated approach to writing and punctuation. But that's okay, because we should write the way we speak. At work we work fast and we speak fast, so accuracy in mechanics should be sacrificed so we can communicate as quickly as possible."

Boss: "Messaging, sure, it might make sense. But email? No way. Every one of your important emails should be as correct and clear as if you had typed out an old-fashioned letter."

If you find yourself thinking hard to justify a habit, ask yourself if you are doing it because you simply don't want to change, or because you truly believe your way of doing things would be highly beneficial to your employer.

COMMAS

How often do you put a period in the wrong place? Or forget to use one? Most likely never. Now ask yourself the same question about the comma. Most people think, "Of course I obey the rules about using the period, but the use of the comma is a subjective thing."

The problem with this reasoning is that there is nothing subjective about it for the reader. If the reader is forced to retrace or falter, even for an instant, then you aren't using commas properly. The four most common problems in using the comma are described below.

Introductory element: Use your ear to decide if a comma is needed after an introductory element; if in doubt, put in the comma.

> unclear: Clueless as always Bob broadcast the email.
> clear: Clueless as always, Bob broadcast the email.

Compound sentence: If two complete sentences are joined by a conjunction, always put a comma in front of the conjunction.

> wrong: Bob broadcast the email but Ben deleted the virus.
> right: Bob broadcast the email, but Ben deleted the virus.

Comma splice: If two complete sentences are joined by a comma, always include a conjunction after the comma.

> wrong: Ann needed office supplies, there were plenty in the cabinet.
> right: Ann needed office supplies, and there were plenty in the cabinet.

Series separator: Always play it safe by putting a comma between every pair of elements in a series. The typical reason for not doing this is the complaint, "Journalists don't do it, so why should I?" Ask them why they do it and they will talk about tradition, not about clarity. You will never be unclear if you include all the commas.

> fuzzy: Amy needed folders, pens and paper.
> clear: Amy needed folders, pens, and paper.

Exercises

Find and fix the errors:

1. Nikola Tesla invented the induction motor but electric resonance was his passion.
2. Charles Steinmetz expanded our knowledge in hysteresis, modeling and lightning.
3. Discovered by Michael Faraday electromagnetic induction electrified the world.
4. Thomas Edison tried his best, his direct-current systems lost out.
5. We went offline at midnight but customers did not notice until noon.
6. The call center needs new telephones, computers and lighting.
7. We went online at noon, five customers called immediately.
8. However many calls remain unanswered.

Solutions

1. Nikola Tesla invented the induction **motor, but** electric resonance was his passion.
2. Charles Steinmetz expanded our knowledge in hysteresis, **modeling, and** lightning.
3. Discovered by Michael **Faraday, electromagnetic** induction electrified the world.
4. Thomas Edison tried his **best, but** his direct-current systems lost out.
5. We went offline at **midnight, but** customers did not notice until noon.
6. The call center needs new telephones, **computers, and** lighting.
7. We went online at **noon, and five** customers called immediately.
8. **However, many** calls remain unanswered.

The Trouble With Commas

Here's the truth: rules about using commas are not really rules, they're guidelines. If you say this near your seventh-grade English teacher, duck or brace yourself for a bit of ear twisting.

Arguments about the use the comma are as old as medieval parchment. For several thousand years, marks that became the modern comma were used to show people reading out loud, or chanting, where best to pause or take a breath. Lately, five hundred years ago or so, they also took on the role of helping to decipher syntax and to decode meaning for those reading silently to themselves. These two uses for the comma have been at war ever since.

Ignore the war. Always start with the "rules" of using the comma. But if something else works better for your situation at work, it's okay to adapt (if your boss approves).

MORE PUNCTUATION

Instead of slogging through long-winded rules for using each punctuation mark, let's review how we use these marks to communicate effectively. Here are important ways we do that:
- Interrupt to explain or emphasize.
- Join complete sentences.
- Join grouped elements.
- Join multi-part nouns.

Interrupt to explain or emphasize.

1. To include an expression that helps explain things, surround it with the comma.

There are, no doubt, good reasons that Dana, their manager, sent the report back.

2. To use an expression that adds a detail but avoid giving it too much emphasis, surround it with parentheses.

We were told by their chief knowledge officer (CKO) that we have until the end of the week (April 17) to approve their report.

3. To add strong emphasis to an interruption, surround it with the em-dash. That's a special dash—as wide as capital M.

We should prepare—before publishing the report—for strong reactions from readers.

(In Word, use [CTRL]+[ALT]+[Num-])

Join complete sentences.

4. If a second sentence explains or illustrates a first sentence, you can join them with a colon.

Orientation leaders need to read the report: it gives details about employee benefits.

5. If you want to show a close relationship between two sentences, you can join them with a semicolon.

Our manager approved the report; the finance department disapproved.

6. If you want to keep related sentences together, and you want to explain the relation a little more, you can join them with a qualifying word such as *however, therefore, consequently,* or *accordingly,* if you surround that word with a semicolon and a comma.

Our manager approved the report; however, the finance department disapproved.

Join grouped elements.

7. To attach a list of things to a thought that contains (or implies) an anticipating expression, such as *these, thus,* or *the following,* that directs attention to that list, use a colon.

These are some of the topics in the report: insurance, training, and pensions.

The report discusses job-related topics: insurance, training, and pensions.

8. To attach a list of things to a thought that anticipates that list, you can join them with an introductory phrase such as *for example, namely,* and *that is,* if you surround that word with a colon and a comma.

The report is used to educate new hires about a variety of topics: for example, insurance, training, and pensions.

9. To join items in a series, where each item already includes a comma, use the semicolon.

The report will be presented by Bob Roberts, director of research; Bill Williams, manager of engineering; and Jimmy James, vice president of operations.

10. To join, yet keep distinct, adjectives that modify the same noun, use the comma.

We wrote a detailed, hard-hitting report.

Join multi-part nouns.

11. To create a compound noun that lacks a noun as one of its elements, use the hyphen.

We got the go-ahead to sell the two-by-fours, but it became a free-for-all.

12. To join the prefix *co* to a word that starts with the letter *o*, use the hyphen (exceptions: *cooperate, coordinate*). If it starts with any other letter, don't use the hyphen.

The co-organizer of our coworkers asked us to cooperate.

13. To join a compound noun that ends with a prepositional phrase, use the hyphen.

The attorney-at-law explained who had the right-of-way.

14. To join a compound noun that shows one person or thing has two functions, use the hyphen.

I asked the realtor-owner to turn on her fax-printer.

Exercises

There is one example for each of these 14 rules of punctuation.

1. The company donates a great deal to charities we care about that is United Way, Habitat for Humanity, and Children's Miracle Network.
2. We need the weekly staff meeting it keeps us all in synch.
3. In addition to being a jack of all trades, Jack is a stay at home dad.
4. They should determine *before* getting the loan the cost of the relocation.
5. The advisors were from different states: Anne Miller, Maine, Larry Horn, Delaware, and Andy Selmer, Illinois.
6. Two large companies are moving to our county therefore unemployment should decrease, and tax revenues should increase.
7. Because he was such a know it all, there was no give and take at the meeting.
8. Four vice presidents all under 40 will discuss career advancement.
9. I am the secretary treasurer on the committee of editor publishers.
10. The following tasks are planned for next week research, write, and edit.
11. A timely surprising email arrived today, and I couldn't be happier.
12. Dana Wilson the main speaker arrived late for the conference.
13. Because the coowner needed to be a co-signer, we needed to coordinate our activities.
14. It's performance has been inconsistent, it's good to see improvement.

Solutions

1. The company donates a great deal to charities we care **about: that is, United** Way, Habitat for Humanity, and Children's Miracle Network. [8]
2. We need the weekly staff **meeting: it** keeps us all in synch. [4]
3. In addition to being a **jack-of-all-trades**, Jack is a **stay-at-home** dad. [13]
4. They should **determine—*before* getting the loan—the** cost of the relocation. [3]
5. The advisors were from different states: Anne Miller, **Maine; Larry** Horn, **Delaware; and** Andy Selmer, Illinois. [9]
6. Two large companies are moving to our **county; therefore, unemployment** should decrease, and tax revenues should increase. [6]
7. Because he was such a **know-it-all**, there was no **give-and-take** at the meeting. [11]
8. Four vice **presidents (all under 40) will** discuss career advancement. [2]
9. I am the **secretary-treasurer** on the committee of **editor-publishers**. [14]
10. The following tasks are planned for next **week: research**, write, and edit. [7]
11. A **timely, surprising** email arrived today, and I couldn't be happier. [10]
12. Dana **Wilson, the main speaker, arrived** late for the conference. [1]
13. Because the **co-owner** needed to be a **cosigner**, we needed to coordinate our activities. [12]
14. **Its** performance has been **inconsistent;** it's good to see improvement. [5]

FINAL COMMENTS

You have no excuse to ever get *its/it's* wrong again in your life. The memory aid, *His, hers, its: no apostrophe fits*, is as easy and helpful as it gets. The author is rather proud of it. He will be disappointed if you don't make it part of your writing arsenal.

It's easy to get caught up in all the interesting effects that can be accomplished with punctuation marks. Try to temper your newfound enthusiasm with the notion that sometimes better writing, and better re-writing, is the preferred way to go. Consider this sentence:

Here at Blazing Eagle Security, we offer trustable, affordable services, at your office, in your home, or in your home office!

Nothing incorrect there. Nothing makes the reader stop to figure out what the heck is going on. However, the reading could be smoother if we forsake the commas for a re-write:

Blazing Eagle Security offers services that are trustable and affordable. You can use them at your office or in your home.

The science of punctuation and the art of clear re-writing can complement each other or substitute for each other.

FAQs

Q: *In several places I found commas without conjunctions in your writing in this book. What's that all about?*

A: I have two answers for you. First, I'm my own boss, so I can do whatever I want. Second, they were written that way on purpose. Sometimes the cadence of a sentence sounds better without the conjunction. This usually only works in shorter sentences. The same goes for comma separators in a series that uses no conjunction: X, Y, Z instead of X, Y, and Z. By not including the conjunction *and*, I can adjust the cadence so that I sound serious or confident. But I try not to overdo it.

Q: *Can't my spell checker find most of these mistakes?*

A: It is helpful if you have a spell checker and grammar checker that spot many of your errors. It would be enough if you're confident your reader doesn't mind working around errors like *your/you're* or *their/they're*. But wouldn't it be better to be viewed as competent rather than sloppy? A good step in that direction is to do a Find Next search for a word that gives you trouble, such as *their*, and verify they are all used correctly. Yes, it sounds tedious, but you'll be surprised how quickly it goes.

Q: *If I'm still unsure about commas, is it better to put too many in or not enough?*

A: Start by using too many commas. Until your writing is as smooth as silk you can rely on commas to guide the reader by marking boundaries between expressions and thoughts. Of course if your boss says, "Hey, cut it out with all the commas," it's time to make do with fewer. Or it's time to start doing some re-writes that don't require as many commas.

CHAPTER 4

Matching Words

> ### *In This Chapter*
>
> - Verbs must match subjects: always.
> - Pronouns must match, or: delays.
> - Modifiers must match, or: confusion.

WHY YOU SHOULD CARE

When you don't make your words match, your readers will unconsciously shudder each time they have to gloss over a verb that doesn't match the subject or a modifier that dangles so badly it looks like a remnant from a prior re-write.

Their brains will hurt, and they will blame you. They might not realize it and they might not know why, but they will. Reading your writing gave them a headache. You made them work harder than they should have had to work.

There is only one solution to this problem: due diligence. You must be diligent in spotting when you use words that don't match. To become a good 'catcher' of mistakes, you have to become a skillful editor. To become a skillful editor, you have to practice. This chapter provides plenty.

VERBS

When readers arrive at a plural verb, but they know the subject is singular, they have to fix the problem mentally while continuing to read. You should spare them that much work. But it isn't easy. First you have to watch for tricky situations:

Tricky situation 1: When two nouns are joined by *or* or *nor*, the noun closest to the verb determines whether the verb should be singular or plural:
>Either her sisters or Amy pays for upkeep.
>Neither Amy nor her sisters eat breakfast.

Tricky situation 2: When what looks like a compound noun is actually the name for a single item, the verb is singular:
>Peaches and cream is on the dessert menu.
>Peaches and cream are in my shopping cart.

Tricky situation 3: When a plural form noun is used in a singular sense, it takes a singular verb:
>Statistics is my favorite subject.
>These statistics refute the hypothesis.

Tricky situation 4: Collective (group) nouns can act as a unit or as separate member:
>The team meets today.
>The team members vote tomorrow.

Tricky situation 5: When a plural form pronoun is used in a singular phrase, it takes a singular verb:
>Most of the work is done.
>Most of the workers are off today.

However, the most common problem is distance: when the verb is way down the sentence, long after the subject. In that case, it's an easy mistake to make the verb match something nearer to it.

Chapter 4 ~ Matching Words   57

MAKE IT A GAME

Let's play a game called Line & Link. Read *quickly* through the paragraph below, following these rules:

1. When you read a noun that appears to be the subject of the sentence or of a clause, underline it with a single line.

2. When you read a verb that looks like the main action of the sentence or clause, underline it with a double line. For a split second consider whether the verb matches the noun you underlined. If it doesn't seem to match it, circle the verb and move on.

Some people find it helpful to mumble nonsense syllables, such as "dah deh dah" or "yada yada," when reading quickly over the words in between the subjects and verbs. Use whatever works for you.

Everyone in the organization, including my colleagues, understand that we want to maintain a learning culture. We believe that it is appropriate for humans to be proactive problem solvers. Each reality and truth about our working environment are pragmatically discovered. Accurate data and relevant information flows freely in a fully-connected network. Human nature, though presumed good for most people, are at least mutable. My group in Marketing and Sales believe that diverse but connected units are good for the organization. We also believe that we must allow for a diversity of task-oriented and relationship-oriented people.

There are seven sentences in the paragraph below. You should have found an error in all but two of the sentences. When you play Line & Link, what you are actually doing is using your ear and your short term memory to isolate and combine subject/verb pairs. In the first sentence, for example, you should have quickly selected and combined, *Everyone understand*, which should have triggered a nasty response from your grammar-trained brain.

Everyone in the organization, including my colleagues, **understands** that <u>we</u> <u>want</u> to maintain a learning culture. <u>We</u> <u>believe</u> that <u>it</u> <u>is</u> appropriate for <u>humans</u> <u>to be</u> proactive problem solvers. **Each** reality and truth about our working environment **is** pragmatically discovered. Accurate **data and** relevant **information flow** freely in a fully-connected network. **Human nature**, though presumed good for most people, **is** at least mutable. My **group** in Marketing and Sales **believes** that diverse but connected <u>units</u> <u>are</u> good for the organization. <u>We</u> also <u>believe</u> that <u>we</u> <u>must allow</u> for a diversity of task-oriented and relationship-orientated people.

Exercise

Use Line & Link to find and fix the errors:

All employees in the organization, including Bob, understands that for a contract to exist there must be an offer, an acceptance, and consideration. An offer is a statement that indicates a willingness to enter into a bargain on the terms stated. Each contract offer proposed by our colleagues are recorded by Ben. Acceptance occurs when the offeree indicates a willingness to accept the bargain proposed by the offeror. Bob and Ben, though normally quick on the uptake like the rest of the staff, often gets confused by the term, offeree. Consideration is anything of value, whether property, promises, or dollars, that are exchanged by the parties. Bob's group in external affairs, also known as public relations, often give consideration in the form of cash.

Solution

All **employees** in the organization, including Bob, **understand** that for a contract to exist there must be an offer, an acceptance, and consideration. An offer is a statement that indicates a willingness to enter into a bargain on the terms stated. **Each** contract offer proposed by our colleagues **is** recorded by Ben. Acceptance occurs when the offeree indicates a willingness to accept the bargain proposed by the offeror. **Bob and Ben**, though normally quick on the uptake like the rest of the staff, often **get** confused by the term, offeree. Consideration is **anything** of value, whether property, promises, or dollars, that **is exchanged** by the parties. Bob's **group** in external affairs, also known as public relations, often **gives** consideration in the form of cash.

PRONOUNS

The purpose of the pronoun is to make the reading go smoothly, by avoiding the repetition of nouns. However, if there is ever any doubt about what a pronoun refers to, the reader must stop for an instant and make a best guess. That's bad. To spot these pronoun problems, it helps to know what to look for. The three most common pronoun errors are:

Limbo: It's not obvious whom the pronoun refers to.
Bob left the office to look for Ben, but <u>he</u> should be easy to reach.
   (To whom does *he* refer?)

Mismatch: The pronoun doesn't match (in person or number) the thing it obviously refers to.
Bob's cubicle was often home to impromptu meetings because <u>they have</u> a water cooler in front of <u>them</u>.
   (The third person singular pronoun is appropriate: *it has .. it*.)

Shift: Bad parallel construction leaves one pronoun different from the others it should be similar to.
Each office had its own hookup to the Internet, a large window that made <u>them</u> bright, and an oak desk that made it elegant.
   (All three phrases should use *it*.)

Exercises

1. The consultants presented a detailed briefing about how it could advise the client.
2. My boss had a conversation with the attorney that caused her to modify her presentation.
3. I liked the creative maneuvering, the competition gunning for you, and the feeling I was in a race to dominate the field.
4. Their programmer had a discussion with our engineer that changed his mind about the action plan.
5. She disliked the office bickering, the need to watch one's back, and the feeling that she was being judged.
6. Our accountant wrote a detailed plan about how it could track expenses.

Solutions

1. The consultants presented a detailed briefing about how **they** could help the client.
2. After talking with the attorney, my **boss modified her** presentation.
3. I liked the creative maneuvering, the competition gunning for **me**, and the feeling I was in a race to dominate the field.
4. Their programmer had a discussion with our engineer that changed **the programmer's** mind about the action plan.

   Their programmer had a discussion with our engineer that changed **the engineer's** mind about the action plan.

   Their programmer had a discussion with our engineer, **who** changed his mind about the action plan.
5. She disliked the office bickering, the need to watch **her** back, and the feeling that she was being judged.
6. Our accountant wrote a detailed plan about how **she** could track expenses.

MODIFIERS

Modifiers are words or phrases that act as adjectives or adverbs. They make our writing more specific, interesting, and memorable. But when badly placed, they can confuse the reader. The most common problems are these four:

Misplaced: It's not put close enough to the words modified.
Bob insisted we stop posting jokes about Ben <u>on the coffee maker</u>.
   (Posting on the coffee maker? Or is Ben sitting on the coffee maker?)

Squinting: It can refer to the words before it or after it.
Bob remembered <u>recently</u> joking about Ben.
   (Recently remembered? Or recently joking?)

Disruptive: It interrupts the reading.
The joke, because Bob insisted we display a modicum of office decorum, was taboo.
   (Are you sure you want to put your reader on hold?)

Dangling: It modifies nothing in particular.
<u>Although a humorless boss</u>, everyone kept telling that joke.
   (Everyone is not the boss. Who is?)

Exercises

1. The electricity, because the utility company was having trouble meeting peak demand, was off for several hours.
2. The accountant said she will need all departments to submit their budgets to her office at a meeting yesterday.
3. As a new employee, his mentor told stories about the early days of the company.
4. Programmers who change code repeatedly frustrate our project managers.
5. Our technicians, because the service had been interrupted for an entire day, had to work overtime.
6. The young consultant presented the report wearing jeans.
7. Despite being written well, my boss talked on and on about how clarity should be the goal of all our correspondence.
8. Customers who call about the service constantly interrupt our technicians.

Entertainers use misplaced modifiers to create humor:

Bert: "Speaking of names, I know a man with a wooden leg named Smith!"

Mary Poppins: "What's the name of his other leg?"

Groucho Marx: "The other day I shot an elephant in my pajamas. (How he got in my pajamas I'll never know.)"

It's okay to make up jokes at work. But try not to become the source of jokes for your misplaced modifiers.

Solutions

1. The electricity was off for several hours, **because the utility company was having trouble meeting peak demand.**
2. **At a meeting yesterday,** the accountant said she will need all departments to submit their budgets to her office.
3. **He was a new employee, so** his mentor told stories about the early days of the company.
4. Programmers who **repeatedly** change code frustrate our project managers.
   Programmers who change code are known to **repeatedly** frustrate our project managers.
5. **Because the service had been interrupted for an entire day,** our technicians had to work overtime.
6. The young consultant **wore jeans when she** presented the report.
7. **Despite the fact that my email was written well,** my boss talked on and on about how clarity should be the goal of all interoffice correspondence.
8. Customers who **constantly** call about the service interrupt our technicians.
   Customers who call about the service are **constantly** interrupting our technicians.

FINAL COMMENTS

When things match, your readers never even notice. That's the goal here: they don't know you did all that editing and re-writing. Your prose is so smooth, they probably assume you write first drafts with perfection. There is no need to disabuse them of that misconception. As Ernest Hemingway said:

> "It's none of their business that you have to learn to write. Let them think you were born that way."

Please note: this doesn't have to be done alone. Making things match, becoming a better editor—it might seem like it's got to be a solo activity. It doesn't have to be. It's easier and more fun to share the effort with a coworker. And it can be your secret.

FAQs

Q: *If I'm using a gender neutral subject, what possessive modifier should I use later in the sentence? For example, should I write: "Ask your friend for his/her opinion of why effective writing is important." OR "Ask your friend for their opinion of why effective writing is important."*

A: Using *his/her* was the first, sometimes awkward, step in the necessary evolution toward gender-neutral writing at work. It has now become preferred practice to use *their* even though the pronoun number (singular versus plural) might be incorrect. Another solution is to change the earlier noun: for example, *friend* to *friends*: "ask your friends for their opinions." Finally, let others weigh in. If something sounds awkward to you, read it to a friend. If they don't frown and stomp their feet, maybe you're overanalyzing.

Q: *English is not my native language, so it's hard to use my ear to find errors in my writing. Is there anything else I can do?*

A: Sorry, but the truth is the people who grew up speaking English have a 20-year head start. Two things make the uphill battle worth it. First, most people are happy to help you learn; simply ask them when you aren't sure how to say something correctly. (And then write it down to review once in a while.) Second, once you do start to catch up and begin to write as easily and as well as native English speakers, you will have a huge advantage over them (especially Americans): you will be truly and fluently bi-lingual.

CHAPTER 5

The Right Words

In This Chapter

- Who/whom? Try using IC-WaWa.
- Use memory aids for homonyms.
- Idiom is learned by hearing it.

WHY YOU SHOULD CARE

Each of the three topics in this chapter is a gnat. Every time a reader glosses over one of these mistakes, that mistake wriggles off the page and morphs into a gnat that flies up and flutters around the reader's head, flops against an eye, threatens to be breathed up the nose, or whines in an ear. Gross, huh?

Distracted readers are unhappy readers. They might not know they're unhappy, but they are. At work, you can't afford to be making people unhappy. You must choose your words wisely, make sure they're the right words. Why? Because we have all been conditioned to be on the lookout for errors in the use of who/whom and homonyms and idiom. The trap is set. Correct word choice is the only way around it.

WHO VERSUS WHOM

Until you're a famous writer or the boss at your company, you should follow the rules for using *who* and *whom*. It's better to play it safe than to gamble by using *who* all the time.

The expert <u>who</u> we hired arrived early.

   (Is *who* correct? Or should it be *whom*?)

Most people have some knowledge about how to choose between *who* and *whom*. Few people have fond memories of having the rules hammered into them in school. We can improve the knowledge and soften the memories by using the IC-WaWa technique.

Step 1: Isolate the Clause (IC) that goes with the word *who* or *whom*.	The expert [who we hired] arrived early.
Step 2: Substitute the word WaWa for the word *who* or *whom*.	The expert [WaWa we hired] arrived early.
Step 3: Re-arrange the words in the clause to make a sentence that states a fact.	The expert [We hired WaWa.] arrived early.

Step 4: If WaWa can be *hi<u>m</u>* or *the<u>m</u>*, then WaWa is an object:
   use *who<u>m</u>* or *who<u>m</u>ever*.

   If WaWa can be *he* or *they*, then WaWa is a subject:
   use *who* or *whoever*.

	The expert [We hired him.] arrived early. { WaWa = *him*, so use *whom* }
Final result:	The expert **whom** we hired arrived early.

Exercises

1. Since you're the boss, you must decide whom should be promoted.

    clause: [_____]

2. The man who you called is asking who's been trying to reach him.

    [_____]

3. They're claiming that you're the one whose job it was to find out who ordered the printer.

    [_____]

4. You're correct in that its their job to speak to whomever calls for assistance.

    [_____]

5. Whom could explain their predicament?

    [_____]

6. Their work schedule changes from week to week, depending on whomever needs time off and who's on vacation.

    [_____]

7. As I said when we were there, the accountants to whom I spoke were aware of your concerns about the program and its finances.

    [_____]

8. I will hire whoever I can find, but they're hiring whomever you suggest.

    [_____]

    [_____]

Solutions

1. Since you're the boss, you must decide [*WaWa(He) should be promoted.*].
   Since you're the boss, you must decide **who** should be promoted.
2. The man [*You called WaWa(him).*] is asking who's been trying to reach him.
   The man **whom** you called is asking who's been trying to reach him.
3. They're claiming that you're the one whose job it was to find out [*WaWa(He) ordered the printer.*].
   They're claiming that you're the one whose job it was to find out **who** ordered the printer.
4. You're correct in that its their job to speak to [*WaWa(He) calls for assistance.*].
   You're correct in that **it's** their job to speak to **whoever** calls for assistance.
5. [*WaWa(He) could explain their predicament.*]?
   Who could explain their predicament?
6. Their work schedule changes from week to week, depending on [*WaWa(He) needs time off.*] and who's on vacation.
   Their work schedule changes from week to week, depending on **whoever** needs time off and who's on vacation.
7. As I said when we were there, the accountants [*I spoke to WaWa(them).*] were aware of your concerns about the program and its finances.
   As I said when we were there, the accountants to whom I spoke were aware of your concerns about the program and its finances.
8. I will hire [*I can find WaWa(them).*], but they're hiring [*You suggest WaWa(them).*].
   I will hire **whomever** I can find, but they're hiring whomever you suggest.

HOMONYMS

Homonyms are words that sound the same but have slightly different spellings and often have very different meanings. The spell checker is not your friend when it comes to homonyms; it can give you a false sense of security about the correctness of your writing. The only solution is diligence. You must be diligent in memorizing how to properly use homonyms, and you must be diligent in looking for them in your writing.

affect: influence (verb) effect: result (noun) effect: cause (verb)	Air affects aardvarks; eels effect electricity.
complement: complete compliment: praise	To complement is to complete.
principle: rule, truth principal: main, chief	A principle is a rule, you fool, A principLE is a ruLE!
adverse: harmful averse: opposed	Avis is averse to adverse ads.
assure: convince ensure: make certain	I assured my assistant, who is since convinced.
continuous: uninterrupted continual: repeated	Our continual ball is in the fall.
discreet: prudent discrete: distinct	When we meet, be discreet.
stationery: paper stationary: fixed	Wary Mary—sat stationary.

A note to English-language purists:

Yes, these aren't all homonyms. Maybe none of them are. Doesn't matter. Homophone, homograph, homonym. We all know what's going on here: we easily type some words wrong because they sound so similar to other words.

A fun brain teaser for word geeks:

Q: What homonym is its own antonym?

A: It means to cut, or separate. It also means to adhere, or attach together. (cleave)

Use it at parties, at your peril.

Exercises

Select the best words:

1. The acquisition will complement/compliment our product line and please our principle/principal investor, but it will also adversely effect/affect morale.
2. Some managers were adverse/averse to our plan to assure/ensure that we would have continuous/continual performance reviews.
3. The signal jumped between several discreet/discrete voltage levels, but the source was stationary/stationery and didn't affect/effect our conclusions.
4. She was complimented/complemented for being so principaled/principled as to assure/ensure that protocol was followed.
5. To avoid adverse/averse management reaction, he was discrete/discreet about ordering the expensive stationary/stationery.

Solutions

1. The acquisition will **complement**/~~compliment~~ our product line and please our ~~principle~~/**principal** investor, but it will also adversely ~~effect~~/**affect** morale.

2. Some managers were ~~adverse~~/**averse** to our plan to ~~assure~~/**ensure** that we would have ~~continuous~~/**continual** performance reviews.

3. The signal jumped between several ~~discreet~~/**discrete** voltage levels, but the source was **stationary**/~~stationery~~ and didn't **affect**/~~effect~~ our conclusions.

4. She was **complimented**/~~complemented~~ for being so ~~principaled~~/**principled** as to ~~assure~~/**ensure** that protocol was followed.

5. To avoid **adverse**/~~averse~~ management reaction, he was ~~discrete~~/**discreet** about ordering the expensive ~~stationary~~/**stationery**.

IDIOM

Idiom is the proper way to say something, because once upon a time it became the accepted way to say something. There are thousands of idiomatic phrases. Don't even try to memorize the few idiomatic phrases below. Read them out loud to let your mind record the sounds of the word combinations.

prepositions before:

among colleagues
between factions

infinitives:

intends to do X
try to see if X

prepositions after:

apologize for X
based on X
bored with X
complied with X
concerned about X
disappointed with X
independent of X
in search of X
modeled on X
plan to X
regarded as X
worried about X

parallels:

associate X with Y
attribute X to Y
both X and Y
compared X to Y (re: similarities)
compared X with Y (re: differences)
distinguish X from Y
not only X but also Y
not so much by X as by Y
not the X but the Y
regard X as Y
so X that it Y
to X is to Y

Examples

Read the sentences out loud and select the best words:

1. Bob should apologize (about/for) the broadcast email.
2. It was logical to associate the new contract award (and/with) our improved proposals.
3. Ann and Amy attribute their success (to/as being from) their new writing skills.
4. Ben's decision to start was based (on/around) his view that Bob would be late.
5. Arguments about bonuses arose (among/between) colleagues and (among/between) factions.

Solutions

1. Bob should **apologize for** the broadcast email.
   → **apologize for X**
2. It was logical to **associate** the new contract award **with** our improved proposals.
   → **associate X with Y**
3. Ann and Amy **attribute** their success **to** their new writing skills.
   → **attribute X to Y**
4. Ben's decision to start was **based on** his view that Bob would be late.
   → **based on X**
5. Arguments about bonuses arose **among colleagues** and **between factions**.
   → **among colleagues**   **between factions**

Exercises

Read the sentences out loud and select the best version:

1. Employees were bored with the cafeteria food.
   Employees were bored of the cafeteria food.

2. The awards were given to both Ben and Amy.
   The awards were given to both Ben as well as Amy.

3. To describe the differences, Bob compared a report to a briefing.
   To describe the differences, Bob compared a report with a briefing.

4. To point out similarities, Ben compared an email to a letter.
   To point out similarities, Ben compared an email with a letter.

5. We were surprised that the CFO complied along with the rules.
   We were surprised that the CFO complied with the rules.

6. Ann was disappointed at the selection of markers.
   Ann was disappointed with the selection of markers.

7. Ben is able to distinguish inkjet from laser.
   Ben is able to distinguish inkjet and laser.

8. Ben's response was delivered independent of Bob's.
   Ben's response was delivered independent from Bob's.

9. Amy went in search for a staple remover.
   Amy went in search of a staple remover.

10. Ben intends to do his exercises while on break.
    Ben intends on doing his exercises while on break.

Solutions

1. Employees were **bored with** the cafeteria food.
   → **bored with X**

2. The awards were given to **both** Ben **and** Amy.
   → **both X and Y**

3. To describe the differences, Bob **compared** a report **with** a briefing.
   → **compared X with Y**   (when focused on differences)

4. To point out similarities, Ben **compared** an email **to** a letter.
   → **compared X to Y**   (when focused on similarities)

5. We were surprised that the CFO **complied with** the rules.
   → **complied with X**

6. Ann was **disappointed with** the selection of markers.
   → **disappointed with X**

7. Ben is able to **distinguish** inkjet **from** laser.
   → **distinguish X from Y**

8. Ben's response was delivered **independent of** Bob's.
   → **independent of X**

9. Amy went **in search of** a staple remover.
   → **in search of X**

10. Ben **intends to do** his exercises while on break.
    → **intends to do X**

Exercises

Read the sentences out loud and select the best version:

1. Bob's report is modeled after Amy's detailed outline.

   Bob's report is modeled on Amy's detailed outline.

2. The briefing is not only 40 pages long but also 10 times as boring.

   The briefing is not only 40 pages long but 10 times as boring.

3. Improved performance was caused not so much by raises but instead by praises.

   Improved performance was caused not so much by raises as by praises.

4. It was not the coffee but the pastry that appealed to Ben.

   It was not the coffee but instead the pastry that appealed to Ben.

5. Does Ann plan to visit the head office?

   Does Ann plan on visiting the head office?

6. Bob and Ben regard the new policies to be winds of change.

   Bob and Ben regard the new policies as winds of change.

7. The email was so critical it caused everyone to get upset.

   The email was so critical that it caused everyone to get upset.

8. To theorize about office culture is applying management science.

   To theorize about office culture is to apply management science.

9. We will try to see if Ben is finished.

   We will try and see if Ben is finished.

10. Amy is not worried about the details of the plan.

    Amy is not worried over the details of the plan.

Solutions

1. Bob's report is **modeled on** Amy's detailed outline.
   → **modeled on X**

2. The briefing is **not only** 40 pages long **but also** 10 times as boring.
   → **not only X but also Y**

3. Improved performance was caused **not so much by** raises **as by** praises.
   → **not so much by X as by Y**

4. It was **not the** coffee **but the** pastry that appealed to Ben.
   → **not the X but the Y**

5. Does Ann **plan to** visit the head office?
   → **plan to X**

6. Bob and Ben **regard** the new policies **as** winds of change.
   → **regard X as Y**

7. The email was **so** critical **that it** caused everyone to get upset.
   → **so X that it Y**

8. **To** theorize about office culture **is to** apply management science.
   → **to X is to Y**

9. We will **try to see** if Ben is finished.
   → **try to see if X**

10. Amy is not **worried about** the details of the plan.
    → **worried about X**

FINAL COMMENTS

We are all handicapped by the comfort of ignorance. Some people around us at work are complacent in their ignorance of proper English. For example:

- They hate the word *whom*, just on general principle.

- They don't use a homonym incorrectly because they made a spelling mistake. They use it incorrectly because they memorized the definition incorrectly years ago. And now they aren't too keen on being corrected.

- They prefer incorrect idioms because, "that's how people talked where I grew up."

Ignore their ignorance. Write correctly. Don't look back.

In the preface to his book *Writing for Results*, David Ewing said:

> "The aim of this book is to remove one major curse that has plagued writing instruction. This is the curse of litany, dullness, patness, pedestrianism. Good writing—that is, writing that persuades or informs as the writer intends—should be personally challenging. It should be as interesting or even as exciting to do as an assignment in marketing or financial analysis or engineering or architecture."

It's an old book but a good book. If you ever see this red hardcover in a used bookstore, grab it. You won't regret it.

FAQs

Q: *'Whom' sounds stuffy to me. Can't I just write 'who'?*

A: Of course you can. Just don't be surprised when 'those people who persist in communicating correctly and clearly' get promoted before you do. But what if your boss is proud of his street smarts and considers the word *whom* to be pretentious? The answer is simple: re-write the sentences so you don't have to use the word *who* or the word *whom*.

Q: *I really do know the difference between homonyms like 'there' and 'their,' or 'here' and 'hear.' But for some reason when I'm writing, I inadvertently type in the wrong word. Any tips for how to avoid this? My spell checker doesn't always find my mistakes.*

A: If the document is important, the best solution is a fresh read; get a friend to proofread your writing. Alternatively, use Find Next to search for all occurrences of those homonyms that haunt you. This will find the mistakes, and the effort will eventually recalibrate your writing mind to make fewer mistakes to begin with.

CHAPTER 6

Department of Corrections

> ***In This Chapter***
>
> - Correctness? You be the judge.
> - Rules, usage, opinions: your choice.
> - Use proofreading tricks, or diligence.
> - Practice with the 15 biggies.

WHY YOU SHOULD CARE

Imagine you've been in your new job for two months. You submit a document and your boss points out two grammar errors in your writing. Now imagine you've been there two years. You submit a document and, again, your boss finds the same two errors. Do you really think your boss would be unfair to conclude that you refuse to change because you just don't care?

It's simple: your writing must use correct English. It's a requirement for your job. Proofread! Use this chapter to practice—and focus on the things you repeatedly get wrong.

JUDGE

Other than my boss, whom should I obey regarding my writing? There is no single authority on good writing. Yes, the dictionary spells things out in black and white. But as the topic moves from spelling to grammar to style, rules become opinions with shades of gray.

In this workbook you will find both rules and opinions. They shouldn't be new to you. School teachers presented most lessons as rules, and colleagues are free with their opinions about how you should write.

The best thing to do is obey the rules and consider the opinions. It's your writing, so you are the sole judge.

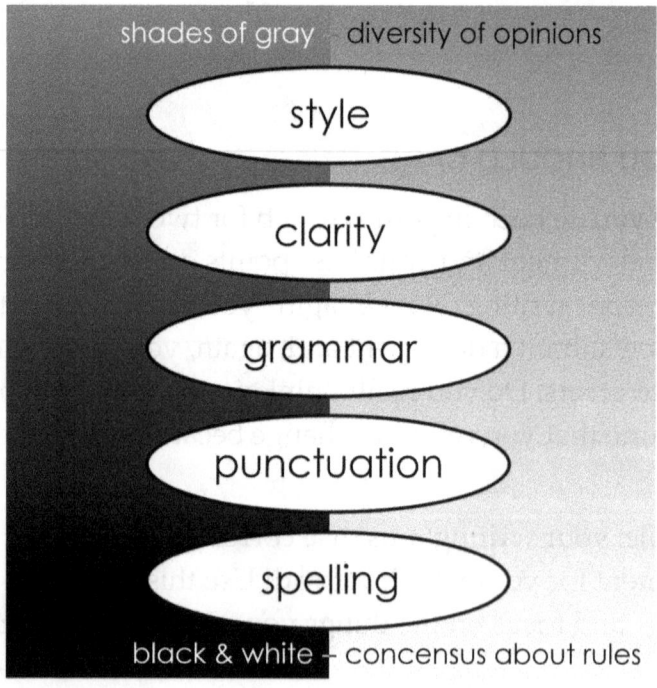

Chapter 6 ~ Department of Corrections   85

However, there is a third source of authority in writing: usage. By this we mean how most people generally use English. And it is not always easy to figure out which authority should be followed. It's like the rock-scissors-paper game:

rock-scissors-paper ↔ rules-opinions-usage

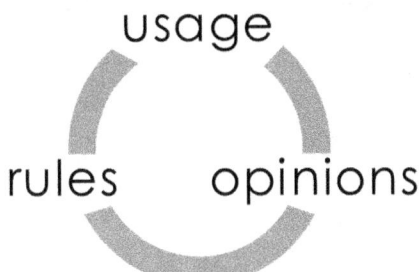

At work, effective communication should outweigh grammatical purity. So, usage usually trumps rules.

Now let's have some fun conjuring clever answers to some brain teasers about rules, usage, and opinions:

Give an example of why the local dictionary is not always the final authority regarding spelling.

___

Describe what Winston Churchill meant when he said: "This is the sort of errant pedantry up with which I will not put."

___

Explain what is wrong with the following pronouncement: "At work, never use a big word when a small word could be used."

___

Solutions

Red is a color in America but a colour in Canada. Also, new words are not in old dictionaries.

Strict adherence to rules of grammar (never end a sentence with a preposition) can make us sound unnecessarily silly.

There are too many exceptions. If we replace "microscopic" with "tiny" our writing becomes less precise.

PROOFREAD

Proofreading is like combing your hair. If you don't do it, you will look sloppy. Your comb, like a spell checker, is necessary but not sufficient. Your mirror doesn't show every part of your head, so you need to find a way to identify every imperfection.

Use a straight edge: Cover up all but the first line of the paragraph below. Circle errors then move to the next line.

I need you're advise. Your my "guru of goop.' Their maybe trouble with the mixture. Should'nt we package it in plastic. Its like mashed potatos. It will travel by plain, than by train.

Go backwards: Point at the final word of the paragraph below. Play "follow the bouncing ball" and go left and then up a line, pointing at every word in reverse order. Circle errors you find.

This work enviroment is like a race coarse it's frantic and loud. Wouldn't you like some piece an quiet. This weak we should'nt be hear. But a brake from the action might be to much to ask four.

How many errors did you find using each technique? There are 12 errors per paragraph, evenly distributed among sentences. Some people find the straight edge technique useful for grammar and the backwards technique useful for spelling. But, to be honest, few people find either technique exceedingly useful. Now you know: *there are no shortcuts.*

Two other simple habits can help:

Use hardcopy: Editing a document on a computer can cause anxiety; we get tense when we spend a lot of time typing on a keyboard and staring at a screen. We edit better when we are relaxed, and we are more relaxed when we sit back and hold paper as we edit the text printed on it.

Ask a buddy: Even the best of friends love to find fault; use it to your advantage.

WATCH FOR THE BIGGIES

How do you make sure your writing is correct? You can use every trick in the book: straight edge, going backwards, using hardcopy, asking a friend. In the end, however, it is your responsibility, so you should strive to be a careful proofreader, if only to find and fix the most common errors.

Here are the top 15 things people forget to watch out for when writing at work:

1. Introductory clauses should be followed by a comma.

    Despite a faltering economy AMF bought more bowling centers.

    Despite a faltering **economy, AMF** bought more bowling centers.

2. Make it obvious what a pronoun refers to.

    AMF declared bankruptcy, but its bowling centers remained open. It surprised bowlers.

    AMF declared bankruptcy, but its bowling centers remained open. **The bankruptcy** surprised bowlers.

3. In a compound sentence with a conjunction, also use a comma.

    Fred Schmidt invented the pinspotter in 1936 and two years later he was hired by AMF.

    Fred Schmidt invented the pinspotter in **1936, and** two years later he was hired by AMF.

4. Check spelling for words that sound the same or sound similar.

    They drank beer, but it didn't effect there score.

    They drank beer, but it didn't **affect their** score.

Chapter 6 ~ Department of Corrections   89

5. Optional modifying words should be set off with commas.

> AMF after its reorganization became profitable again.
>
> AMF, **after its reorganization**, became profitable again.

6. In a compound sentence with a comma, also use a conjunction.

> AMF's pinspotter debuted in 1946, it sparked a revolution in the bowling industry.
>
> AMF's pinspotter debuted in 1946, **and** it sparked a revolution in the bowling industry.

7. Watch for the tricky apostrophes with plural possessives.

> Most bowling center's revenues kept growing, as did participation in childrens leagues.
>
> Most bowling **centers'** revenues kept growing, as did participation in **children's** leagues.

8. Avoid shifting from one verb tense to another.

> More than 100 million people will bowl each year, so bowling was a good business.
>
> More than 100 million people **bowl** each year, so bowling **is** a good business.

9. Avoid shifting from one kind of pronoun to another.

> When one first enters an AMF bowling center, you are impressed by the colorful décor.
>
> When **you** first **enter** an AMF bowling center, you are impressed by the colorful décor.

10. Make the verb match the subject in number.

> The bowlers on our team is sure to win. Each of the bowlers practice once a week.
>
> The bowlers on our team **are** sure to win. Each of the bowlers **practices** once a week.

11. Use commas to separate all items in a series.

> AMF operates bowling centers around the world: 36 in Australia, 9 in Mexico and 5 in Japan.
>
> AMF operates bowling centers around the world: 36 in Australia, 9 in **Mexico, and** 5 in Japan.

12. Make each pronoun match its noun in number.

> Each of the 518 bowling centers will operate on their regular schedule.
>
> Each of the 518 bowling centers will operate on **its** regular schedule.

13. The possessive for *it* does not use an apostrophe, but *it is* does.

> Its good that its bowling centers remained open.
>
> **It's** good that its bowling centers remained open.

14. Follow an introductory modifier with the thing it actually modifies.

> Bowling in a league, scores improve if beer drinking is limited.
>
> Bowling in a league, **you** improve if beer drinking is limited.

15. Keep parallel things parallel.

> The league bowler arrived early, drinks beer, and has fallen over.
>
> The league bowler arrived early, **drank** beer, and **fell** over.

Note: Admittedly there is some repetition between this activity and other lessons in this book. That's not a bad thing. Practice makes perfect.

Chapter 6 ~ Department of Corrections

Exercise

A coworker is writing a report on the Professional Bowlers Association (PBA). She has asked you to proofread two paragraphs from her first draft. Find and fix all mistakes in her prose, editing for correctness only.

Entrepreneurs from Microsoft bought the PBA and they soon made significant changes. To start with, they recruited new corporate sponsors, including Motel 6, Denny's and Ace Hardware. Three other big changes were made by the PBA: it rewarded winners in a unique way, it increases tournament prize money, and it expanded it's membership. Top bowlers excepted stock options. Wanting to entice new members, the overall prize fund grew to $9 million. Membership grew to 4,250, and sources say they will soon exceed 5,000. Also, sideline coaching was banned, the dress code was relaxed. This upset some bowlers, who had assumed that this would not change.

What would it be like to bowl in the PBA Open? To begin with you must pay an entry fee of $500. To compete, you need skills similar to those of top bowlers. These competitors, the best in the world typically score above 200. You need precise control to conquer the flat oil pattern on the lanes. To win, you need a miracle, though its most bowler's dream. When one makes it to the final rounds, your called a casher, because than you have been competing for the $375,000 in prize money. The top four players in the tournament is shown live on ESPN.

Hint: If you find more than 18 errors, you could be accused of being overzealous.

Solution

Entrepreneurs from Microsoft bought the **PBA, and** [3] they soon made significant changes. To start with, they recruited new corporate sponsors, including Motel 6, **Denny's, and** [11] Ace Hardware. Three other big changes were made by the PBA: it rewarded winners in a unique way, it **increased** [15] tournament prize money, and it expanded **its** [13] membership. Top bowlers **accepted** [4] stock options. Wanting to entice new members, **the PBA** [14] **increased** the overall prize fund to $9 million. Membership grew to 4,250, and sources say **it** [12] will soon exceed 5,000. Also, sideline coaching was **banned, and** [6] the dress code was relaxed. **The ban on coaching** [2] upset some bowlers, who had assumed that this would not change. {9 errors}

What would it be like to bowl in the PBA Open? To begin **with, you** [1] must pay an entry fee of $500. To compete, you need skills similar to those of top bowlers. These competitors, **the best in the world,** [5] typically score above 200. You need precise control to conquer the flat oil pattern on the lanes. To win, you need a miracle, though **it's** [13] most **bowlers'** [7] dream. When **you make** [9] it to the final rounds, **you're** [4] called a casher, because **then** [4] you **are** [8] competing for the $375,000 in prize money. The top four players in the tournament **are** [10] shown live on ESPN. {9 errors}

FINAL COMMENTS

Proofread? Who has time to to proofread? I send out dozens of emails every day. I send out even more replies, though their usually brief. I write a detailed status update every few days. And I write weakly progress reports. It should be enough that the software I use checks for errors in spelling and grammar as I type. Apparently its not.

How far into that paragraph did you get before you realized what was going on? There's a mistake in every other sentence.

That software you rely on isn't all-knowing, so you can only trust it so far. Your mind isn't perfect, so your eyes will deceive you. Solicit the assistance of another sense: read it out loud. And if it's really important stuff, beg a friend and coworker to embarrass you by finding all the errors.

FAQs

Q: *Whenever I'm not sure about grammar, I pull out my old school books. When the topic is style, I refer to this new book I bought. I also use a dictionary and a thesaurus. It's a lot of books to deal with. Why isn't there a single book I can refer to for most issues?*

A: Actually, there is. Go get a copy of *The Gregg Reference Manual*. Some people look at it and think, "Oh, that's just for secretaries and typists." They are wrong and small minded. It is as comprehensive and authoritative as it gets. If you've got money to burn, go buy a new copy of the latest version. Otherwise, a second hand copy of the ninth or tenth edition will do. The latest versions are typically different because of changes in technology available to people writing at work. You don't need that. What you need is the timeless advice about all those writing topics:

Part 1: Grammar, Usage, and Style
Punctuation . Capitalization . Numbers . Abbreviations . Plurals and Possessives . Spelling . Compound Words . Word Division . Grammar . Usage
Part 2: Techniques and Formats
Editing . Proofreading . Memos . Email . Reports . Manuscripts . Notes and Bibliographies . Tables . Other Business Documents . Forms of Address
Part 3: References
Glossary of Grammatical Terms . Pronunciation Problems . Rules for Alphabetic Filing . Index

The most useful section is the last: this 600-page book has a 20-page Index where each page has three columns and all the text is small but readable.

Q: *I wrote this report. High-level people are going to read it. I did my best and proofread it. I even asked a friend to help and she did. But I'm wondering, is it okay to pay someone to proofread it for me? Or is that somehow cheating?*

A: No, it's not cheating. It's your life. It's your job. It's your money. Many companies hire independent proofreaders for important documents. If you do, then you're saving your company money.

SECTION III

Making it Effective

Let's say you get everything correct: spelling, punctuation, grammar, and vocabulary. Now you know you're not going to turn people off with mistakes. You still have to turn them on to your message. Correctness is merely the price of admission. Effectiveness is another world entirely, and it's subjective stuff. Give it thought, give it a try. You'll learn what works for you.

Chapter 7: In Search of Clarity – Did you ever get to the end of a paragraph and think, "Wait, what was that all about?" The writing was not clear. Yours will be, because you will learn how to cut words, replace words, and keep your story clear.

Chapter 8: Good Behavior – It's easy to write with negativity, bias, bluster, and ego. But you can behave better than that, and you should. Practice editing your words so that readers aren't distracted or insulted by those four sins of lazy writing.

Chapter 9: Words with Impact – At work, brevity matters. You need to say a lot with the fewest number of words. One way to get there is to use the pyramid of concise writing.

Chapter 10: Easy Reading – Have pity on your reader: make your writing easy to read. Use active voice and parallel constructions. Guide the reader with transitions and links. Surprise the reader with variety in your sentences.

~ Subject in Action ~

Riley was a bright, organized, and well-liked new employee. No one was surprised when Riley became the team leader for a small project just months after coming on board. Consensus was that she was the right person for the job.

Riley was conscientious about communicating with her team. A mentor had told her, "You can never over communicate." Initially, her team was responsive and happy to be kept in the loop. But after a while, Riley observed that despite her frequent and detailed emails, her team often didn't know information essential to getting the project done. In fact, it appeared that some team members didn't even receive her messages. She checked the distribution on her emails to verify that everyone was on it.

Finally, Riley met privately with a team member to ask what was going on. He admitted that he didn't read a lot of what Riley sent out. It took too much time to sift through all the words and too much effort to figure out the key points. He and most of the team had given up trying.

It was a good wake-up call for Riley. After that, she continued to maintain open communication with her team, but she was careful to share information more concisely and with a better focus on things of most importance. Her effort was rewarded with a higher performing project team.

CHAPTER 7

In Search of Clarity

> **In This Chapter**
>
> - Choose clarity, or get un-chosen.
> - Trim the unnecessary and redundant.
> - Conflicted verbs need replacing.
> - Align grammar to the story.

WHY YOU SHOULD CARE

As a new employee, you must write clearly. Coworkers will quickly discount your value if all they do is frown and scratch their heads when they read what you wrote. No matter who you are, you must admit that you're not perfect, that you can write more clearly. In a way, your goal should be that your coworkers improve *their* productivity. When you help them spend less time deciphering your words and less time in wasted effort because they misunderstood your writing, you become the person who helps get things done, the one who leads because everyone clearly understands.

CLARIFY

Below are two examples of academic writing—abstracts for research papers. On the line below each example, complete the sentence with two or three words to summarize the issue for a CEO who has been advised to implement the idea proposed in the research paper.

This paper investigates how an organization facilitator should organize a production activity in which multiple units produce different components where each unit has private information about its cost. When informational decentralization prevails and scheduling optimization is a function of the sum of the marginal costs of the different components, the facilitator should prefer informational consolidation to informational decentralization.

    1. It explains how to _____ .

Game theory and common sense both support the notion that, in the context of repeated negotiations, it helps to establish a reputation for "toughness." If you can get and keep this reputation, then others will anticipate tough play and respond accordingly, yielding benefits that outweigh the costs. Effective yet ethical means to achieve this reputation are explained in the following pages.

    2. It explains how to _____ .

Which one of these examples was easier to read? If you had to choose one of the authors based on their writing, who would you hire to advise you?

Ponderous writing is a problem in most professions: academia, science, engineering, medicine, law, etc. Unfortunately, it is not just a bad habit that practitioners inherit. It is often considered part of the moral code within each profession. John Kenneth Galbraith said it well:

> "Complexity and obscurity have professional value: they are the academic equivalents of apprenticeship rules in the building trades. They exclude outsiders, keep down the competition, preserve the image of a privileged or priestly class. The man who makes things clear is a scab. He is criticized less for his clarity than for his treachery."

Some employers and bosses insist that you write unclearly on purpose. But if you do have a choice, edit for clarity, not for conformity to the ponderous style of others in your profession.

WORDINESS

Your readers are just like you: they are busy people, and they don't have all the time in the world. They want to get to the main point of your message quickly. So avoid wordiness. There are three things you can do when editing:

Delete deadwood.

Get rid of words and phrases that are unnecessary. For example, there is seldom a good reason for beginning a sentence with *I should mention that*. The same goes for the phrase *It has come to our attention that*.

Sandblast bloat.

Replace fancy words and phrases with simple equivalents. For example, you can usually replace *indication* with *sign*, and *banking facility* with *bank*. We're used to hearing phrases like *at this point in time*, but we all know the writer means *now*. Why not just say it?

Uncover buried verbs.

This is most easily done by spotting words that end with *-ion*. For example, *make a suggestion* can often be replaced by *suggest*. You can probably guess what verbs should be used instead of abstract nouns like *formation, representation,* and *mitigation*.

Chapter 7 ~ In Search of Clarity

Exercises

Delete deadwood.

1. This letter is to advise you that your office is in the process of being cleaned; it should also be noted that extra work is required to be carried out on the carpets and drapes.

2. I should mention that in order to change our contract it is a fact that you need both signatures.

Sandblast bloat.

3. In order to make it to the finalization of the project, you will need financial resources for emergency situations.

4. To establish approval of the contract, it is necessary that you peruse its contents and subsequently administer your signature.

Uncover buried verbs.

5. We have a suspicion that if you make a recommendation for leniency, they will come to the conclusion that our plan is not to raise an objection.

6. He needed an implementation of a checking account so that he could remit compensation for his utilization of our program that enables interactions with the network.

Solutions

1. ~~This letter is to advise you that~~ your office is ~~in the process of~~ being cleaned; ~~it should also be noted that~~ extra work is required ~~to be carried out~~ on the carpets and drapes.

2. ~~I should mention that in order~~ to change our contract ~~it is a fact that~~ you need both signatures.

3. To **finish** the project, you will need **money** for **emergencies**.

4. To **approve** the contract, **read** it then **sign** it.

5. We **suspect** that if you **recommend** leniency, they will **conclude** that our plan is not to **object**.

6. He needed **to implement** a checking account so that he could **compensate us when he utilized** our program that **interacts** with the network. [okay, sort of]

    He needed **to start** a checking account so that he could **pay** for his **use** of our program that **interacts** with the network. [better]

UNNECESSARY WORDS

When we use unnecessary words, we distract or bore the reader. Always strive to remove deadwood, such as the phrase *the purpose of* in the following sentence:

Government reports are useful for ~~the purpose of~~ showing bad writing at work.

Exercises

1. The letter was improved by means of a well-written purpose.
2. Amy used to think that surrounding circumstances precluded her from finishing.
3. A table describing the results does not have to be absolutely complete.
4. One necessary condition for good writing is an assessment of the reader.
5. The graphs were drawn in the same way as described in the lesson on charts.
6. We had various discussions about our next rollout.
7. Ann could not successfully escape the need to be a diplomat.
8. Ben's critiques about the outline were few in number but helpful.
9. Usage is found to be as important as rules or opinions.
10. I should make mention of the lack of clarity in academic writing.
11. However, alignment is needed in cases where you want to be clear.
12. It is often the case that I forget to distribute the agenda.
13. Use at least one out of the three ways to vary sentence format.
14. Few people outside of our department approved his recommendations.
15. It's good that Bob will plan ahead to coordinate the review.

Solutions

1. The letter was improved by ~~means of~~ a well-written purpose.
2. Amy used to think that ~~surrounding~~ circumstances precluded her from finishing.
3. A table describing the results does not have to be ~~absolutely~~ complete.
4. One ~~necessary~~ condition for good writing is an assessment of the reader.
5. The graphs were drawn ~~in the same way~~ as described in the lesson on charts.
6. We had ~~various~~ discussions about our next rollout.
7. Ann could not ~~successfully~~ escape the need to be a diplomat.
8. Ben's critiques about the outline were few ~~in number~~ but helpful.
9. Usage is ~~found to be~~ as important as rules or opinions.
10. I should ~~make~~ mention ~~of~~ the lack of clarity in academic writing.
11. However, alignment is needed ~~in cases~~ where you want to be clear.
12. ~~It is~~ often ~~the case that~~ I forget to distribute the agenda.
13. Use at least one ~~out~~ of the three ways to vary sentence format.
14. Few people outside ~~of~~ our department approved his recommendations.
15. It's good that Bob will plan ~~ahead~~ to coordinate the review.

MORE UNNECESSARY WORDS

Exercises

1. Ben thinks it's more preferable to put a comma between every pair of elements in a series.

2. Writing is not refined in nature if it includes misplaced modifiers.

3. Directors and administrators are not one and the same.

4. Passive voice is acceptable in five separate situations.

5. For sentences that are small in size, wordiness is seldom a problem.

6. Learn to delete deadwood so that in the future you will not have a problem with wordiness.

7. It's important to understand the fact that participation is mandatory.

8. Describe each new type of thing with precise details.

9. In order to avoid negative reactions, don't use words like *avoid*.

10. The most unique thing about our plan is its simplicity.

11. Avoid buzzwords until such time as you can use them judiciously.

12. I warned them in advance to remove the legalese.

13. I have my own particular way of avoiding vanity in my lucid prose.

14. Bob is not sure as to whether the sample was representative.

15. You can find the best word with the aid of a good style manual.

Solutions

1. Ben thinks it's ~~more~~ preferable to put a comma between every pair of elements in a series.

2. Writing is not refined ~~in nature~~ if it includes misplaced modifiers.

3. Directors and administrators are not ~~one and~~ the same.

4. Passive voice is acceptable in five ~~separate~~ situations.

5. For sentences that are small ~~in size~~, wordiness is seldom a problem.

6. Learn to delete deadwood so that ~~in the future~~ you will not have a problem with wordiness.

7. It's important to understand ~~the fact~~ that participation is mandatory.

8. Describe each new ~~type of~~ thing with precise details.

9. ~~In order~~ to avoid negative reactions, don't use words like *avoid*.

10. The ~~most~~ unique thing about our plan is its simplicity.

11. Avoid buzzwords until ~~such time as~~ you can use them judiciously.

12. I warned them ~~in advance~~ to remove the legalese.

13. I have my own ~~particular~~ way of avoiding vanity in my lucid prose.

14. Bob is not sure ~~as to~~ whether the sample was representative.

15. You can find the best word with ~~the aid of~~ a good style manual.

REDUNDANT PHRASES

When we use phrases that are partly redundant, we distract or confuse the reader. Always strive to remove redundancies, such as the words *a time of* in the phrase *a time of two hours* in the following example:

Ben spent ~~a time of~~ two hours responding to the email.

Exercises

1. The email generated a total of 28 responses.
2. Most people responded and asked the question, "Why did I get this email?"
3. For the message, Ben assembled together his thoughts about training.
4. However, concern about the email was brief in duration.
5. A rumor began to circulate around that all emails were being recorded.
6. The consensus of opinion was that the email was appropriate.
7. The consensus was that each and every letter was beginning to look like a report.
8. The resultant effect is that salutations are becoming optional.
9. Enclosed herewith is a report about our training needs.
10. Use only true facts to support your claims.
11. One of the basic fundamentals of writing a résumé is to keep it brief.
12. No two résumés are exactly identical.
13. His second job was managing foreign imports of electronics.
14. She described the new innovations she introduced as training coordinator.
15. Keywords should be an integral part of a résumé submitted online.

Solutions

1. The email generated ~~a total of~~ 28 responses.
2. Most people responded and asked ~~the question~~, "Why did I get this email?"
3. For the message, Ben assembled ~~together~~ his thoughts about training.
4. However, concern about the email was brief ~~in duration~~.
5. A rumor began to circulate ~~around~~ that all emails were being recorded.
6. The consensus ~~of opinion~~ was that the email was appropriate.
7. The consensus was that ~~each and~~ every letter was beginning to look like a report.
8. The ~~resultant~~ effect is that salutations are becoming optional.
9. Enclosed ~~herewith~~ is a report about our training needs.
10. Use only ~~true~~ facts to support your claims.
11. One of the ~~basic~~ fundamentals of writing a résumé is to keep it brief.
12. No two résumés are ~~exactly~~ identical.
13. His second job was managing ~~foreign~~ imports of electronics.
14. She described the ~~new~~ innovations she introduced as training coordinator.
15. Keywords should be ~~an integral~~ part of a résumé submitted online.

MORE REDUNDANT PHRASES

Exercises

1. If we join together the purpose, statements, and ending, we have the core of an announcement.

2. In my opinion I think this letter will survive the Embarrassment Test.

3. Ann's hopeful optimism was evident in her presentation.

4. During the period from 2008 to 2012 our department archived 400 reports.

5. Archiving the reports requires advance planning for file space.

6. Bob's report suggested that, at a price of $1000, the computers were a bargain.

7. The report described our forward progress with the drug testing.

8. All diagrams in the report were rectangular in shape.

9. To convince legislators, a necessary requisite is the willingness to demonstrate.

10. The end result is a law we can live with.

11. The headline should be no more than one sentence in length.

12. We drove to the meeting at a rate of 60 miles per hour.

13. The bullet points summarize the present status of the projects.

14. Amy's presentation lasted for a duration of three hours.

15. At the end of the presentation, she turned in the direction to face the president.

Solutions

1. If we join ~~together~~ the purpose, statements, and ending, we have the core of an announcement.

2. ~~In my opinion~~ I think this letter will survive the Embarrassment Test.

3. Ann's ~~hopeful~~ optimism was evident in her presentation.

4. ~~During the period~~ from 2008 to 2012 our department archived 400 reports.

5. Archiving the reports requires ~~advance~~ planning for file space.

6. Bob's report suggested that, at ~~a price of~~ $1000, the computers were a bargain.

7. The report described our ~~forward~~ progress with the drug testing.

8. All diagrams in the report were rectangular ~~in shape~~.

9. To convince legislators, a ~~necessary~~ requisite is the willingness to demonstrate.

10. The ~~end~~ result is a law we can live with.

11. The headline should be no more than one sentence ~~in length~~.

12. We drove to the meeting at ~~a rate of~~ 60 miles per hour.

13. The bullet points summarize the ~~present~~ status of the projects.

14. Amy's presentation lasted for ~~a duration of~~ three hours.

15. At the end of the presentation, she turned ~~in the direction~~ to face the president.

BUREAUCRATIC VERBS

When a verb phrase uses more words than it needs to use but only hints at what it really wants to say, it's acting like a bureaucrat. Here is an example:

Ann's diagram <u>is an illustration of</u> how to fill out the form.

This sentence speaks with force and clarity if we unleash the descriptive power of the real verb:

Ann's diagram **illustrates** how to fill out the form.

Exercises

1. On our Internet connection, peaks in traffic are in excess of 2 Mbps.
2. Next year's budget is dependent on last year's performance.
3. The employees' contention is that the pension fund is in jeopardy.
4. Each section title contains a hint at what comes next.
5. Casual Fridays had an effect on office moral.
6. Ann achieved the establishment of her plans for next year.
7. Amy will accomplish orientation of new hires.
8. Our department manager made a decision to accelerate performance reviews.
9. The sales department makes predictions for increased revenues each quarter.
10. Bob's boss will make reports on our progress.
11. In her presentation, she provided a description of the plan of action.
12. Our users' manual makes provisions for simplifying how to use the software.
13. Mr. Smith will give consideration to going to Washington.
14. The negotiation failure occurred because neither side would compromise.
15. Each cubicle is provided with two file cabinets.

Solutions

1. On our Internet connection, peaks in traffic **exceed** 2 Mbps.
2. Next year's budget **depends on** last year's performance.
3. The **employees contend that** the pension fund is in jeopardy.
4. Each section title **hints at** what comes next.
5. Casual Fridays **affected** office moral.
6. Ann **established** her plans for next year.
7. Amy will **orient** new hires.
8. Our department manager **decided to** accelerate performance reviews.
9. The sales department **predicts** increased revenues each quarter.
10. Bob's boss will **report on** our progress.
11. In her presentation, she **described** the plan of action.
12. Our users' manual **simplifies** how to use the software.
13. Mr. Smith will **consider** going to Washington.
14. The negotiation **failed** because neither side would compromise.
15. Each cubicle **has** two file cabinets.

CONFLICTED VERBS

When we use a generic verb that has multiple meanings we leave it up to our readers to decide which sense, or personality, of the verb is the proper one.

The policy <u>covered</u> new employees for major medical expenses.

The verb *cover* can mean *conceal, clothe, insure, deal with,* or *report details*. Thus, in the reader's mind the word *cover* might cause confusing associations with alternate definitions. To avoid this, substitute a lean verb that says what we really meant:

The policy **insured** new employees for major medical expenses.

Exercises

Cross out conflicted verbs and suggest replacements.

1. The unacceptable budget represents our biggest problem.
2. By being observant, Amy acquired a better understanding of office politics.
3. Bob and Ben wanted to achieve their best.
4. After the workshop, they employed their new skills to rewrite that proposal.
5. Ann's writing illustrates how to use parallel construction.
6. Using email, she supplied a reminder about the upcoming meeting.
7. The email also presents information about prior meetings.
8. The meeting is likely to terminate after the vote on the amendment.
9. We accomplished the survey with great difficulty.
10. After three meetings, we determined that the policy was flawed.
11. All supervisors will soon initiate their performance reviews.
12. In his report, Ben established that our conclusions were wrong.
13. Bob wonders whether the report exhibits enough data.
14. Bob and Ben both utilize inexpensive cell phones.
15. Please describe the speech you will perform at the offsite meeting.

Solutions

Your answers may be different but appropriate. It depends on how you interpreted each sentence.

1. The unacceptable budget ~~represents~~ our biggest problem. → **is**
2. By being observant, Amy ~~acquired~~ a better understanding of office politics. → **gained**
3. Bob and Ben wanted to ~~achieve~~ their best. → **do**
4. After the workshop, they ~~employed~~ their new skills to rewrite that proposal. → **used**
5. Ann's writing ~~illustrates~~ how to use parallel construction. → **shows**
6. Using email, she ~~supplied~~ a reminder about the upcoming meeting. → **sent**
7. The email also ~~presents~~ information about prior meetings. → **gives**
8. The meeting is likely to ~~terminate~~ after the vote on the amendment. → **end**
9. We ~~accomplished~~ the survey with great difficulty. → **finished**
10. After three meetings, we ~~determined~~ that the policy was flawed. → **concluded**
11. All supervisors will soon ~~initiate~~ their performance reviews. → **start**
12. In his report, Ben ~~established~~ that our conclusions were wrong. → **proved**
13. Bob wonders whether the report ~~exhibits~~ enough data. → **has**
14. Bob and Ben both ~~utilize~~ inexpensive cell phones. → **use**
15. Please describe the speech you will ~~perform~~ at the offsite meeting. → **make**

Exercise

That was fun. Let's try some more. The following paragraph is a bit scatter-brained. But if you replace the conflicted verbs, each sentence becomes a bit more clear.

Yesterday we implemented the new testing system. It institutes new methods within the Civil Service department. Applicants no longer indicate their answers on booklets. Instead, test stations were furnished with touch screens. This necessitates that users adapt. They shouldn't have too much trouble operating the program. But they should take their time formulating their answers to the essay questions. A blinking icon denotes that time is running out. All personal electronic devices must be eliminated from the work space. Remember: what transpires in test room stays in test room.

Solution

Yesterday we **put into use** the new testing system. It **introduces** new methods within the Civil Service department. Applicants no longer **mark** their answers on booklets. Instead, test stations were **equipped** with touch screens. This **requires** that users adapt. They shouldn't have too much trouble **using** the program. But they should take their time **framing** their answers to the essay questions. A blinking icon **means** that time is running out. All personal electronic devices must be **removed** from the work space. Remember: what **happens** in test room stays in test room.

HERE'S THE BIG STUFF

To really make your writing clear:

- Align grammar to the story.
- Grab the reader's attention with actions.

Align grammar to the story.

Every sentence we write is being read twice: in the reader's brain there is a grammar reader and a story reader. The grammar reader follows the structure of the sentence. The story reader follows the meaning of the sentence. Alignment occurs when the grammar matches the story, and it's this alignment that makes a sentence 'more clear'. Here is the breakdown of grammar and story for a misaligned sentence:

not the easiest to read: A decision was made by the Mint to keep the penny.

grammar:	subject:	decision	verb:	was made
story:	actor:	Mint	action:	decided

Using the story, rewrite the sentence to get the aligned, and therefore clear, version:

story:	actor:	Mint	action:	decided
grammar:	subject:	Mint	verb:	decided

clear: The **Mint decided** to keep the penny.

To create alignment:

1. Identify the actor (person or thing) and make it the subject.
2. Identify the action of the actor and make it the verb.
3. Rewrite the sentence using the new subject and verb.

Another example:

Creation of a large plaster model is done by an artist, then reduction of the image onto a steel master hub is accomplished by a Janvier lathe.

   actor: _artist_   action: _creates_   actor: _lathe_   action: _reduces_

An **artist creates** a large plaster model, then a Janvier **lathe reduces** the image onto a steel master hub.

And another, rather famous, example:

Crude oil was spilled by the tanker owing to the fact that mistakes were made.

   actor: _tanker_   action: _spilled_   actor: _captain_   action: _made mistakes_

The tanker spilled crude oil because the captain made mistakes.

Grab the reader's attention with actions.

1. Avoid puffery.
2. Avoid abstractions.
3. Avoid distractions.
4. Avoid announcements.

1. Avoid puffery: choose simple verbs instead of complex ones.

   [bad]   The US Mint utilizes zinc to implement the penny.

   (good)   The US Mint **uses** zinc to **make** the penny.

Verbs should be action words that grab the attention of your reader. When they are unnecessarily complex, they can alienate your reader, and they can convey subtle extra meanings. For example, the word *utilize* suggests "ingenuity in putting to profitable use" and the word *implement* suggests "providing the means to carry out." Neither of these meanings is appropriate in this case.

2. Avoid abstractions: show the real action.

[bad] Inflation <u>is an explanation for</u> the decline of the penny.

(good) Inflation **explains** the decline of the penny.

The real action is in the lively verb *explains*. Try not to hide your action verbs inside abstract nouns formed with generic verbs such as *be*, *do*, or *make*.

3. Avoid distractions: eliminate unneeded verbs.

[bad] The diagrams <u>presented</u> below show production rates for the one-cent coin.

(good) The **diagrams below** show production rates for the one-cent coin.

A verb that is not really needed in a sentence still grabs the attention of the reader. The result is misplaced emphasis.

4. Avoid announcements: keep attention on the action.

[bad] <u>It is</u> the blanking press <u>that</u> makes the planchets.

(good) The blanking press **makes** the planchets.

When you begin a sentence with *It is* or with *There is*, you often reduce verb power, because you emphasize other elements of the sentence, usually the subject.

Exercise

Edit the text below to make it more clear.

The penny should be eliminated. Consideration has been given by Congress to bills that would terminate production of pennies. The main problems are rising costs and decreasing usefulness:
- The Mint employs metals with unpredictable prices.
- The government spends 1.4 cents to fabricate each penny.
- There are few vending machines that accept pennies.

These facts illustrate that the penny is not needed. The table located in the next section is a list of further reasons to eliminate the penny. The conclusion by staffers was that Congress should act.

Preservation of the penny is needed. There are predictions by economists that abandoning the penny would hurt the poor. Other reasons to keep the penny are:
- Rounding to the nickel would escalate prices.
- It is historical fact that the Mint earns $20 million a year on pennies.
- Most people exhibit a fondness for the penny.

Coinstar did a survey of the public and found that 65% of respondents favored maintaining the penny in circulation. See the data given in the next section for more details.

Solution

The penny should be eliminated. **Congress has considered** bills that would **end** production of pennies. The main problems are rising costs and decreasing usefulness:

- The Mint **uses** metals with unpredictable prices.
- The government spends 1.4 cents to **make** each penny.
- **Few vending machines accept** pennies.

These facts **show** that the penny is not needed. The **table in** the next section **lists** further reasons to eliminate the penny. **Staffers concluded** that Congress should act.

The penny should be **preserved. Economists predict** that abandoning the penny would hurt the poor. Other reasons to keep the penny are:

- Rounding to the nickel would **raise** prices.
- **The Mint** earns $20 million a year on pennies.
- Most people **are fond of** the penny.

Coinstar **surveyed** the public and found that 65% of respondents favored **keeping** the penny. See the **data in** the next section for more details.

PLAIN WORDS ON CLARITY

To always achieve the greatest clarity, wouldn't it make sense to always use the simplest words and the shortest sentences?

If your only goal is 'no reader left behind' then sure, it makes sense. Otherwise, you can't go wrong adopting guidelines from the Plain English movement:

1. Use words your readers will understand.
2. Make the average sentence length less than 18 words.

Let's consider some writing we all deal with: legal words on a contract. More specifically, a cancellation policy. Here is a prime opportunity for unscrupulous businessmen to take advantage of people by confusing them with convoluted language. (e.g., credit card companies)

Convoluted version: (average words per sentence: 36)

This service continues and renews annually until such time as either party cancels it which requires that the customer contact the local branch office at the number provided on the reverse side of this invoiced communication.

Simple version: (average words per sentence: 6)

This service goes every year. You don't have to renew it. You can cancel at any time. To cancel, call our office. The number is on the front of this letter.

Clear version: (average words per sentence: 12)

This service will continue, year after year, until you or we cancel. To cancel call your local branch at the telephone number shown on the front side of this letter. You may cancel your program at any time. But be sure to request and receive a cancellation number.

When you are not required to use mind-numbing legalese, use instead easily-understood terms for your coworkers and your customers. In many cases, it's the ethical thing to do.

FINAL COMMENTS

Clear writing is achieved by giving the reader the real story without abstractions or distractions. Coworkers need to get other things done; they want to minimize the time it takes to read and understand. The ideal result is when they don't even realize they read what you wrote. They read it, understood it, acted on it, and moved on with their day at work. Clarity clears the way. It's that simple.

FAQs

Q: *During a busy day at work, who really has time to edit their writing to this level of clarity?*

A: Everyone does. It won't always be a time-consuming activity of editing and re-editing. Over time your first drafts will be closer to your final edits. Eventually, and you might not even notice this, your thinking will become more clear and helpful, all because you put the effort into making your words clear.

Q: *Okay, but what about when I'm writing something that's important. I need the extra words and the formal phrases to make things perfectly clear. No?*

A: No. You don't need a lot of formal words to write important things. Only 462 words were needed to add the Bill of Rights to the Constitution—and that was written by lawyers.

CHAPTER 8

Good Behavior

> **In This Chapter**
>
> - Find alternatives to negative words.
> - Nix words that make you sound biased.
> - Minimize the use of mumbo jumbo.
> - Talk with and about your reader.

WHY YOU SHOULD CARE

Wouldn't it be nice if all your coworkers were upbeat, evolved, honest, and selfless? Of course. And they all feel the same way, so it's up to you to show how it's done, starting with your writing. Keep in mind that your writing does not yet come with personal videos like at Hogwarts. Until it does, your words are all you have to convey your message while also comforting the reader with the social graces that keep all of us from over-reacting to perceived slights and from making unfortunate judgments based on misperceptions. A little effort goes a long way. Imagine your next performance review including kudos for a writing style that puts people at ease.

NEGATIVITY

Negative words: Certain words can trigger negative reactions in the mind of the reader. We begin to sound pessimistic or even mean when we frequently use words with negative connotations, such as these:

allege	deny	ignorant	never	terrible
avoid	disapprove	impossible	no	trivial
bad	eliminate	inadequate	not	trouble
careless	error	inferior	problem	unfair
cease	exclude	lack	prohibit	unreliable
complain	fail	mistake	refuse	weakness
demand	fault	neglect	reject	wrong

negative: If you fail to pay this amount within 30 days, we will demand the balance and eliminate your account.

positive: Your account will stay open if you pay within 30 days.

Negative phrasing: This can hurt our relationships with coworkers. It can lead them to view us as inflexible or rude. If you see that kind of reaction in their eyes, take a step back, take a breath, and use words you might expect from a sweet old grandmother.

negative: You did that wrong.

positive: Please let me show you another way to do that.

Multiple negations: To comprehend a negative, people first imagine the positive and then cancel it out. Doing this too often, especially within one sentence, obscures meaning.

confusing: Interview not more than one candidate unless we haven't closed our hiring window.

clear: If we are not hiring, interview one candidate only.

Exercises

For the sentences below, underline the negative words and then rewrite the sentence. Obviously this is subjective.
Be creative and polite.

We demand that you cease complaining that the alleged problem was our fault.

The odds for new business are terrible if we keep making the same mistakes.

Rewrite these sentences using positive phrasing.
Be encouraging and give suggestions or options.

You didn't provide the necessary information, and we can't start the analysis until we get your input.

That won't work in our company.

Rewrite these sentences without the negations:

Managers should not ask for increased budgets unless they spent not less than 90% of last year's money.

Under no circumstances should you not remind Bob to avoid careless mistakes.

Solutions

We <u>demand</u> that you <u>cease</u> <u>complaining</u> that the <u>alleged</u> <u>problem</u> was our <u>fault</u>.

We **hope** that you **will work with us so** that the **incident** can be **explained.**

The odds for new business are <u>terrible</u> if we keep making the same <u>mistakes</u>.

The odds for new business are **good** if we **improve** our processes.

Please provide your input so **we can proceed** with the analysis. If there's **anything we can do to help**, let us know.

Another way might work in our company. For example …

Managers **may ask for increased budgets if they spent more than 90% of last year's money.**

Always remind Bob to **be careful.**

Chapter 8 ~ Good Behavior   127

All silliness aside, there are circumstances where negative words, and even double negatives, are appropriate. The most important examples involve adding *emphasis* to a statement made in defense of oneself or another:

No, I did not say that.

Ben would never, never do that.

When things go wrong, or even worse when lawyers get involved, the emphasis of extra negative words can help establish, beyond a shadow of a doubt, where you stand or what you meant by what you said.

BIAS

Until the 1920s, women could not vote in the United States. Until the 1970s, women were barred from many jobs. Until our descendants do not frown at the phrase *she or he*, our language will continue to subtly exclude women from equal consideration. Gender bias problems include:

Pronouns: Avoid overusing the politically correct phrases *he or she* and *his or her*. Instead, use a plural pronoun, or rewrite the sentence. A plural pronoun with a singular subject is becoming accepted usage when it's used to avoid gender bias. Our society is bending the rules because it's the right thing to do.

> awkward: The meal he or she orders should fall within his or her budget.
>
> intelligible: The meal they order should fall within their budget.

Occupations: Use an official replacement, or make one up.

businessman	→	executive	fireman → firefighter
salesman	→	salesperson	mailman → mail carrier
congressman	→	representative	foreman → supervisor
policeman	→	police officer	woman attorney → attorney

Name Differences: Be consistent with your references.

> Mr. Tan and his wife Amy → Mr. and Mrs. Tan
> Adam Lee and Ms. Eve Ward → Adam Lee and Eve Ward

People as a Group: Replacements are not hard to find.

> mankind → people, humanity
> man-made → synthetic
> man-hours → work-hours
> common man → average person

Are you rolling your eyes? Do you think this is all ancient history? Just a bunch of unnecessary words for political correctness? You're right, and you're absolutely wrong. It's history in that it was a contentious subject when your parents were growing up. But it's very real. Any psychologist will tell you: *words matter*. The bias they cause can be subtle and even unintended, but it doesn't change the fact that continued use of 'male-gender foremost' terms directly contribute to continued downgrading of women's status, capabilities, and pay.

In addition to gender, there are other forms of bias to avoid, including race, age, sexual orientation, disability, and body size. The list grows as our society evolves. The only constant is the need for sensitivity and a willingness to change.

Exercises

Remove the gender bias in these sentences:

Woodrow Wilson and his wife Edith agreed: the common man would be better off if every congressman voted his conscience about the 19th amendment.

According to Ms. Amy Tan and Bob, every salesman should record his man-hours of effort.

Remove all possibilities of bias from these sentences:

Our young male nurse will meet with the black lawyer and the 52-year-old deaf engineer.

I may be having a blonde moment, but I thought we just hired a kid named Srinivasan, who's probably a whiz at software.

Solutions

Edith and Woodrow Wilson agreed: the **average person** would be better off if **representatives** voted **their** conscience about the 19th amendment.

According to **Amy** and Bob, every **salesperson** should record **their work-hours** of effort.

Our nurse will meet with **the lawyer** and **the engineer**.

I may **not remember this correctly**, but I thought we just hired **someone named** Srinivasan.

DRIVEL

It's okay to spice up your writing at work. Just don't overdo it. A modicum of spice is just right when cooking; too much can ruin the meal. When you edit your first drafts, always be on the lookout for the worst forms of drivel:

Common Clichés: These are accepted, and even expected, by readers of newspapers. They are even acceptable in your writing at work. What is not acceptable is overusing them.

    in hot water   (in trouble)   run of the mill   (typical)

Corporate Clichés: These are verbal shortcuts we use at work. Too often, however, people use them to hedge their commitments by not being clear. Try not to do that.

    touch base   (talk)   push back   (resistance)

Legal Mumbo Jumbo: It's natural to feel the need to write like an attorney when writing something important at work—it's what we're exposed to in the important documents at home, such as contracts. If you're not an attorney, avoid the temptation to write like one.

    cease and desist   (stop)   until such time as   (until)

Corporate Mumbo Jumbo: If you overuse trendy business words, you're likely to look both pompous and desperate. Maintain reader respect by avoiding this dismal drivel.

    leverage   (use)   incent   (give incentives for*)

---

*yes, there are alternatives:
entice, encourage, exhort, impel, incite, induce, motivate, spur, stimulate, urge, …

Exercises

Edit the sentences below, getting rid of the drivel.

1. Heads will roll if we don't go back to ground zero, hunker down, and pull out all the stops to crank it out.
2. Let's take this offline and hash out that disconnect to make sure we're on the same page vis-à-vis the project schedule.
3. Pursuant to our prior conversation re the report it was deemed necessary to attach herewith the appendix per your request.
4. As an evangelist for the new paradigm, my value add is in incenting others to think outside the box.

Solutions

1. **We will be in trouble** if we don't **start over, work hard,** and **finish**.
2. Let's **talk later** and **investigate** that **misunderstanding** to make sure we **agree** on the project schedule.
3. **Here is the appendix.**
4. I **help** by **encouraging** others to think **creatively**.

VANITY

When you use a personal tone in an email or letter, you can make almost any subject more interesting to the reader. Also, when you write about the reader, not about yourself, you make your message truly engaging.

Always remember that your reader will be thinking:

- Why should I care about reading this?
- What does it have to do with me?

To help make the reader interested in what you have to say, write with two techniques in mind:

Converse: Have a conversation with the reader.

> standoffish: It is our pleasure to introduce our new service.
> conversational: You really might like our new service.

Mirror: Make the reader the subject of your sentences.

> writer-oriented: We appreciate the efforts extended on our behalf.
> reader-oriented: Thank you for helping.

Exception: The use of the word *you* should be avoided when it could have a connotation of blame. In this case, change the focus to talk about groups or things:

> reader-focus: You must not include sensitive information in your email.
> group-focus: Employees must not include sensitive information in their email.
> thing-focus: Email must not include sensitive information.

Do you think this is overdoing it? Being so concerned with making the reader the subject of your sentences? Consider this quote by Dale Carnegie, someone who spent much of his life studying how people can get along better:

> "Remember that a person's name is to that person the sweetest and most important sound in any language."

He wasn't kidding. Think about it. If your name is Bob, there's a difference between hearing, "Hey, good morning," and hearing, "Hey, good morning, Bob." It feels better.

Putting it in practice

Jake wondered why he felt hesitant to use people's names at work when talking to them or writing to them. He suspected it had something to do with a huge fight he had had years ago with his absentee father about not calling him 'dad'. He decided to try an experiment. Starting with his emails, he consciously tried to use the pronoun 'you' and people's names as often as he could. This helped ease him into doing the same thing in face-to-face conversations.

At first he couldn't tell if his efforts were having any effect. The proof came during a break in a design review with their biggest client. He overheard the client's program manager say to his boss, "I wish you could get Jake to teach our engineers his age how to lighten up, how to just talk and communicate and get outside their own heads and have more fun at work." Jake's boss responded cautiously, "Jake's too busy, and he's not looking for a new job thank you very much."

But back in the office, Jake's boss began to talk to him about plans and choices for career advancement.

Could this be you?

Exercise

The email below uses unnecessary formality and a writer-oriented focus. Rewrite the sentences in a way that is both conversational and reader-oriented. A good way to do this is to pretend you're sitting with the reader, talking things over.

To:	Wilson, Amy
From:	Breckenridge, Robert
Subject:	Our seminar
Message:	Hello,
	I would like to extend an invitation to an upcoming seminar to learn about our services.
	We put effort into streamlining our presentation so that your time will be well spent.
	Call us if we can answer any questions you might have.
	Respectfully,
	Bob Breckenridge

Solution

To: Amy Wilson

From: Bob Breckenridge

Subject: Please join us

Message:
Amy,

You're invited to a seminar about our services.

Your time is valuable, so we streamlined our presentation.

And **please do call** with any questions; we're here to help.

Regards,

Bob

FINAL COMMENTS

If you are new to your first job, some of these suggestions for 'be nice' wording may seem overdone. Give it a year. In all likelihood you'll look back with chagrin at those times (maybe only a few) where your choice of words contributed to people dismissing your usefulness, or complaining about your attitude, or aggravating turf wars between coworkers.

Social graces count. Few organizations hand out Congeniality Wordsmith Awards. But they all reward employees who get things done, which is often a direct result of putting people at ease with the way you use your words.

FAQs

Q: *Is it ever appropriate to write with negative words? For example, if you keep having a problem with someone, won't you get more attention if you're a little negative than if you keep being polite and positive?*

A: Two answers here. First, the goal in this chapter was not to advise you to be positive instead of negative. It was to advise you to use words that are less likely to instill a negative feeling in the reader. The result isn't happy-pill prose, it's straightforward, clear, emotion-free writing. Second, dealing with a difficult person is a topic worthy of an entire book, and there are plenty out there (books, that is). A few suggestions are worthy of your consideration. If the person just doesn't seem to listen, go ahead and experiment with the emotional power of negative words. Proceed with caution, though. If the person doesn't care what you want, or takes pleasure in thwarting your efforts, written negative words won't do much good. It's time to verbally address the problem by asking your boss for advice about it. If the person is nasty, consider the ideas in the chapter on diplomacy.

Q: *I feel like I need to use "corporate mumbo jumbo" to fit in my organization. If I don't, will it sound like I haven't adapted to my employer's culture? But if I do, will my coworkers make fun of me?*

A: If you overdo it, your coworkers will probably make fun of you. If you refuse to do it, some people will view you as aloof or not a team player. Suggestions: Learn to parrot back a bit of it when *speaking* with important people who use it, but in your *writing* avoid it or find slightly different ways to say it, even if it means using a few more words here and there.

Q: *Political correctness drives me crazy. Isn't avoiding a word like "mankind" overdoing it?*

A: For this issue, it can help to replace the phrase *political correctness* with the phrase *social decency*. And if this topic drives you crazy, it might be a good time to sit back, take a breath, try to relax. Philosophically, this can be a turning point in your life. Are you going to evolve? Or are you going to calcify? Ten years pass. Twenty, then thirty. Along the way, will you allow yourself to have fun participating? Or instead, will you persist in pontificating your rightness? Will you be fascinated by the changes brought about by each generation? Or will you be a judgmental grouch? The choice is rather stark. Choose well.

CHAPTER 9

Words with Impact

> **In This Chapter**
>
> - Every word counts.
> - Trim, shape, and color.
> - Say much, with few words.
> - Use the pyramid of concise writing.

WHY YOU SHOULD CARE

First of all, word count matters. If you are verbose on the page, you spend more time writing and editing, and your readers spend more time trying not to fall asleep. In most jobs, brevity is a virtue. Second, wouldn't you prefer to spend your time getting things done than writing about them? Every hour spent writing is an hour not spent working on something else. Learning to write leaner will free up your time to be more productive on more assignments. Third, people who write concisely live happier, healthier lives, with less anxiety and all the other dysfunctions of the modern world. Mere speculation? Clueless psycho-babble? You decide.

EVERY WORD COUNTS

Many people believe they need to use a lot of words to make their writing good. This is backwards. At work, time is money, so we should make our writing concise. It should state much but use few words. Here is the six-part pyramid to concise writing:

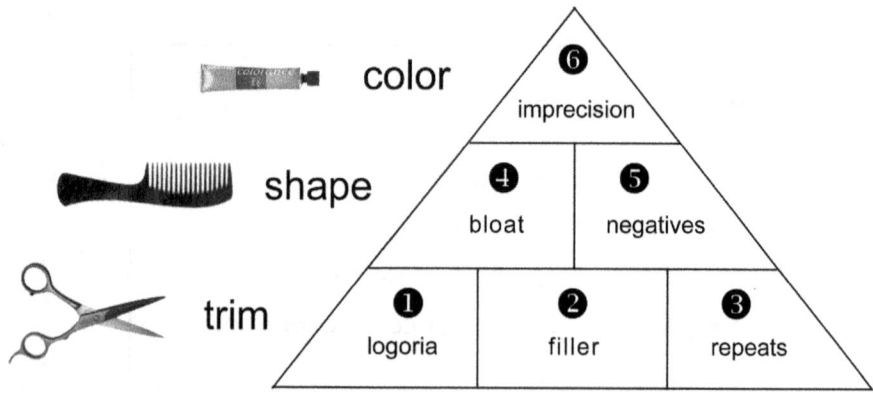

Edit your first drafts to make your final drafts concise, using three levels on the pyramid:

    concise final draft
        ↑
    color   Highlight sentences with vivid details.
        ↑
    shape   Comb phrases to make them clear.
        ↑
    trim   Cut unnecessary words.
        ↑
    wordy first draft

Chapter 9 ~ Words with Impact   141

❶   trim: logoria

Delete any distracting, uncontrolled flow of words at the beginning of a sentence:

The point I would like to make is that ... I must point out that ... I would stress that ...	(Hey, listen to *me*.)
It should be pointed out that ... It goes without saying that ... It should be noted that ...	(Hey, pay attention.)
This letter is to advise you that ... The fact of the matter is that ... It could be argued that ...	(Hey, get a lawyer.)

❷   trim: filler

(a) Delete *qualifiers* that don't say much:

Chris was ~~very~~ aware that the ~~little~~ trouble we had was ~~rather~~ unfortunate.

(b) Delete *identifiers* that don't add much:

The supervisor ~~who is~~ in charge wrote a report ~~that was~~ about overtime charges ~~which were~~ filed last month.

(c) Delete *modifiers* that don't clarify much:

That ~~particular~~ service was ~~actually~~ expanded because ~~various~~ customers have ~~pretty much~~ gravitated to shopping online for ~~virtually~~ all their holiday gifts.

Other culprits:

basically	generally	kind of	sort of
certain	given	practically	specific
definitely	individual	really	type of

❸ trim: repeats

(a) Delete repetitive parts of *pairs*:

Each ~~and every~~ salesperson verified that orders were ~~true and~~ accurate.

Keep the word that is most appropriate to the sentence.

Other culprits:

| any and all | first and foremost | various and sundry |
| one and only | over and done | hope and trust |

(b) Delete *categories* when they are already implied:

My desk will be neat ~~in appearance~~ if the computers are small ~~in size~~.

Other culprits:

~~of a~~ course ~~texture~~	eight ~~in number~~	~~in a~~ confused ~~state~~
extreme ~~in degree~~	area ~~of psychology~~	period ~~in time~~
unusual ~~in nature~~	~~of~~ cheap ~~quality~~	heavy ~~in weight~~

❸   trim: repeats   (continued)

(c) Delete *modifiers* that are already implied by the meaning of the word they modify:

If we continue ~~on~~, the ~~end~~ result could be a ~~terrible~~ tragedy.

The following story is full of unnecessary modifiers:

We stayed late ~~in order~~ **to** help Ben assemble the report.
Working as a team was ~~more~~ **preferable** to burdening him.
Of course, better ~~advance~~ **planning** could have helped.
But we figured ~~joint~~ **cooperation** was the way to go.
We all knew the ~~surrounding~~ **circumstances** were difficult.
There were ~~various~~ **differences** in format and style.
Grammar gaffs ~~continue to~~ **remain** a problem.
And we weren't sure ~~as to~~ **whether** the graphs were done.
There was always the ~~potential~~ **opportunity** for disaster.
But we were confident the ~~final~~ **outcome** would be good.

However, we didn't **anticipate** ~~in advance~~ data file problems.
We worked hard to **merge** ~~together~~ the spreadsheets.
The data was needed **for** ~~the purpose of~~ validating results.
Readers need to **have** ~~at hand~~ supporting facts.
We provided them **adequate** ~~enough~~ background data.
This extra effort **prolonged** ~~the duration of~~ our work.
Next time we will **plan** ~~ahead~~ to order pizza.
It was obvious that **each** ~~individual~~ worker was hungry.
In the end, there was **consensus** ~~of opinion~~ about the report.
When we **cooperate** ~~together~~ like this, we succeed.

❹ shape: bloat

Many bloated phrases can be replaced with a word:

It is crucial that you verify the computer has the ability to reboot.

You **must** verify the computer **can** reboot.

Other culprits:

as regards in reference to concerning the matter of	→	**about**
despite the fact that regardless of the fact that notwithstanding the fact that	→	**although**
the reason for due to the fact that owing to the fact that	→	**because**
prior to in advance of in anticipation of	→	**before**
is able to has the ability to is in a position to	→	**can**
in the event that if it should happen that under circumstances in which	→	**if**
cannot be avoided it is necessary that it is essential that	→	**must**
on the occasion of in a situation in which under circumstances in which	→	**when**

There are many other examples:

subsequent to	→	**after**
afford an opportunity	→	**allow**
am of the opinion	→	**believe**
with reference to	→	**concerning**
decrease in	→	**fewer**
am in receipt of	→	**have**
of considerable magnitude	→	**large**
along the lines of	→	**like**
in close proximity	→	**near**
take cognizance of	→	**note**
at this time	→	**now**
involve the necessity of	→	**require**
the reason for	→	**why**

❺   shape: negatives

Try to change 'not X' phrases to 'Y' words to make your writing more condensed and direct:

<u>Do not accept</u> the report if it is <u>not longer</u> than 150 pages.

Reject the report if it is **shorter** than 150 pages.

Other typical culprits:

not present	→	**missing**	not worried	→	**confident**
not admit	→	**deny**	not the same	→	**different**
not allow	→	**prevent**	not just a few	→	**many**
not often	→	**seldom**	not out of the question	→	**possible**

❻ color: imprecision

Being concise means saying much with few words. If you focus only on minimizing word count, you wind up being laconic, which might be a source of pride for you, but it risks making things ambiguous for the reader.

(a) Sometimes you should change a word to *be more specific*:

A <u>study</u> <u>determined</u> job satisfaction at our <u>facility</u>.

A **survey measured** job satisfaction at our **office**.

(b) Sometimes you should add words to *be more informative*:

Job satisfaction increased.

Job satisfaction increased **by 25%**.

Chapter 9 ~ Words with Impact   147

Exercise

Edit the following section from a business report. Work your way up the pyramid, but only do the first two levels:

1. Delete logoria, filler, and repeats.
2. Reduce bloat and rewrite negatives.

The hotel had been open for years before managers observed that most calls to housekeeping were to request ironing boards. The fact of the matter is that this particular discovery prompted the idea of introducing ironing boards in each and every guest room, at a cost of $40,000. One manager took cognizance of the fact that the budget included $44,000 to replace black-and-white television sets with color sets which were in the bathrooms of VIP suites. Further analysis showed that not one VIP guest had ever requested a non-black-and-white set for their bathroom. It goes without saying that the managers adopted ironing boards instead of color televisions owing to the fact that the advantageous benefits were rather tangible: a $4000 budget surplus, better productivity in housekeeping, and a new feature in each individual guest room.

Hint: Shoot for about a dozen edits.

Solution

The hotel had been open for years before managers observed that most calls to housekeeping were to request ironing boards. ~~The fact of the matter is that~~ [1] This ~~particular~~ [2c] discovery prompted the idea of introducing ironing boards in ~~each and~~ [3a] every guest room, at a cost of $40,000. One manager ~~took cognizance of the fact that~~ **noted** [4] that the budget included $44,000 to replace black-and-white television sets with color sets ~~which were~~ [2b] in the bathrooms of VIP suites. Further analysis showed that ~~not one~~ **no** [5] VIP guest had ever requested a ~~non-black-and-white~~ **color** [5] set for their bathroom. ~~It goes without saying that~~ [1] The managers adopted ironing boards instead of color televisions, ~~owing to the fact that~~ **because** [4] the ~~advantageous~~ [3c] benefits were ~~rather~~ [2a] tangible: a $4000 budget surplus, better productivity in housekeeping, and a new feature in each ~~individual~~ [3c] guest room.

Final Exercise and Solution

To be concise, be precise. Change words to be more specific; add words to be more informative. Here are a few examples:

The **Chicago Marriott** [6b] hotel had been open for **15** [6b] years before managers ~~observed~~ **discovered** [6a] that **65% of** [6b] calls to housekeeping were to request ironing boards. This discovery prompted the idea of ~~introducing~~ **placing** [6a] ironing boards in every guest room, at a cost of $40,000. One manager noted that the budget included $44,000 to replace black-and-white television sets with color sets in the bathrooms of VIP suites. Further ~~analysis~~ **investigation** [6a] showed that no VIP guest had ever requested a color set for their bathroom. So the managers ~~adopted~~ **chose** [6a] ironing boards instead of color televisions, because the benefits were tangible: a $4000 budget surplus, ~~better~~ **increased** [6a] productivity in housekeeping, and a new **and valued** [6b] feature in each guest room.

Still don't get the "add to be concise" idea? Imagine you are a movie producer who has just finished and named a movie, *When They Met*. Nice short title, right? Only three words. But wait, this title can be more concise with four words, *When Harry Met Sally*. It's more concise because it says a lot more, despite being only a little longer.

FINAL COMMENTS

The purpose of this chapter was to walk you through one way of editing, step by step, to a result that is clear and concise. You will develop your own way of trimming your writing. Your effort now and in the near future will lay the groundwork for years of easier writing that actually makes for easier reading.

FAQs

Q: *My manager pointed out to me that I often start sentences with "I think that..." or "In my opinion..." For example, I might write something like, "I think that sales would improve if we did a little more market research." He says I should just say, "Sales would improve if we did a little more market research." And he says that starting with phrases like "I think" makes me sound tentative. I think not using these phrases makes me sound bossy. Who is right?*

A: Your boss is right. The "I think" is implied in every statement we make. This advice can be useful to you. If I had written, "I think this advice can be useful to you," and I did that for all my answers to the FAQs in this book, what good would that have done for you or for me? Let's be honest, not a lot. When you omit the "I think" you do not sound bossy to others. You sound direct and confident. That's a good thing at work.

CHAPTER 10

Easy Reading

> **In This Chapter**
>
> - Active voice makes reading easy.
> - Parallels make comprehension easy.
> - Transitions and links guide the reader.
> - Sentence variety keeps readers awake.

WHY YOU SHOULD CARE

This is a golden rule kind of thing. Do you want to read long-winded, passive-voice writing that's monotonous to the point of torture? Neither does your reader, so don't phone it in. Work hard on the writing so the reading will be easy.

In this chapter you will see how action, parallels, guides, and variety can make the reading less like work and more like an interesting adventure. No, it's not trying to turn you into a novelist or a script writer for children's television. It's helping you train yourself to recognize opportunities to make things smoother, easier, and more interesting for the reader.

ACTIVE VOICE

"Use active voice!" is the mantra of most teachers of clear writing. It's good advice, but how do we do this while editing? There are three ways to change passive voice to active voice:

passive:	doee {is|was|..} Xed by doer	
	Ann was asked by Bob.	**transpose**
active:	doer Xed doee	**the subject**
	Bob asked Ann.	
passive:	in the A the B {is|was|..}Xed	
	In the file the job was listed.	**extract the**
active:	the A Xed the B	**subject**
	The file listed the job.	
passive:	it {is|was|..} Xed that C	
	It was decided that Ben must go.	**supply the**
active:	someone Xed that C	**subject**
	We decided that Ben must go.	

Notice how passive voice forces us to write sentences that are longer and convoluted. If it takes you two seconds to comprehend a sentence written in active voice, it will typically take you three seconds to comprehend the same sentence when it's written in passive voice.

Use passive voice sparingly and in certain situations:

doer is unimportant:	The network will be monitored.
doer is confidential:	The file was destroyed accidentally.
doer is unknown:	The system can be hacked.
to avoid being blunt:	The network crash was caused by his emails.
to maintain flow:	... These activities create a corrupted file. Corrupted files are isolated by network administrators ...

Chapter 10 ~ Easy Reading

Exercises

Transpose the subject:

1. A problem with the server was isolated by Ben.

2. Rationalization of expenditures for office supplies by administrators is necessary to cut costs.

Extract the subject:

3. In the access logs the source of the problem was identified.

4. Within the cabinet a paucity of supplies was revealed.

Supply the subject:

5. It was announced that the server had crashed.

6. It will be explained how the office will continue to function.

Solutions

1. **Ben isolated** a problem with the server.

2. **Administrators must rationalize** expenditures for office supplies to cut costs.

3. **The access logs identified** the source of the problem.

4. **The cabinet revealed** a paucity of supplies.

5. **She announced** that the server had crashed.

6. **He will explain** how the office will continue to function.

PARALLELS

Parallel construction is to prose what rhyme is to poetry. At least that's one way of looking at it. Readers are accustomed to having the benefits of parallel construction: fewer words, improved readability, and easier comprehension.

A common rule of grammar and rhetoric is that when we have groups of similar elements, we should coordinate them by assembling them side by side using a common grammatical structure.

    chaotic: Bob <u>ate</u> lunch, <u>drinks</u> coffee, and <u>has fallen</u> over.

    parallel: Bob **ate** lunch, **drank** coffee, and **fell** over.

Parallel construction should be used in a variety of ways: at the micro level (among clauses), at the intermediate level (among sentences), and at the macro level (among paragraphs and sections).

Exercises

In the sentence below, two predicates are presented, but their structure is not parallel. It is much easier to read when they are similar in structure. Make it so.

The committee recommends spending the surplus on an office party and that next year's budget for entertainment expenses be increased.

In the next example, the items in the lists should be grammatically parallel. If one element of a list is a complete sentence and it reads okay, then all elements should be complete sentences using a similar form. Make things parallel by rewriting bulleted items as imperatives.

To request a change from last year's budget, follow proper procedures:
- Standard form only
- Include a detailed description.
- Your request should be submitted by Tuesday.

The rules of behavior in the park are as follows:
- On arrival, the rangers want you to register.
- Pack out as much as you pack in.
- Only designated areas for camping.
- At night, your food is to be locked up.

The final example is not just for parallel structure, but also for parallel thought. One of the elements in the sentence below is a thought that is not similar to the thoughts in the other elements. Break it out as a new sentence.

The auditor discovered mistakes in accounts receivable, found receipts that had not been recorded, corrected several ledger entries, and all this time our accountant could not be found.

Solutions

The committee recommends spending the surplus on an office party and **increasing** next year's budget for entertainment expenses.

To request a change from last year's budget, follow proper procedures:
- **Use only the standard form.**
- Include a detailed description.
- **Submit your request by Tuesday.**

The rules of behavior in the park are as follows:
- **Register with the rangers on arrival.**
- Pack out as much as you pack in.
- **Camp only in designated areas.**
- **Lock up your food at night.**

The auditor discovered mistakes in accounts receivable, found receipts that had not been recorded, **and** corrected several ledger **entries. All this time** our accountant could not be found.

ENGAGE

To keep the reader engaged, write every "beginning" to entice the reader, over and over again. Each beginning—title, abstract, heading, initial sentence in a paragraph—should hook the reader. It should describe where we are going. Here are some of the actions that hook readers:

- Make a prediction.
- State a definition.
- Give a summary.
- Quote someone.
- Ask a question.
- Tell a story.

A good way to develop the ability to write hooks is to pretend you are writing the words for a roadside billboard. It must be brief, and it must grab the attention of the speeding reader.

Assume the sentence below summarizes a section in a report. Now assume you need to write a heading for that section. Write pithy hooks that capture some of the essence of the sentence. Try to use fewer than nine words for each one. Creative thinking will help you write enticing beginnings.

General Frank explained that the After Action Review (AAR) is a professional discussion of an event, focused on performance standards, that enables participants to discover what happened, why it happened, and how to sustain strengths and improve on weaknesses.

Prediction: _____

Quote: _____

Story: _____

Definition: _____

Cover this up while you work:
Truth will be revealed at the AAR.
"AAR tells it like it is." -General Frank
The general let'em have it at the AAR.
AAR – a candid forum with decorum

GUIDE

Does it flow? Is it easy to follow? These are subjective issues. But because they are important to your reader, they should be important to you. Two simple techniques can help:

Transitions: Between related paragraphs, place a transition sentence to connect them.

> amplify: Repeat a key word or set of words.
> ... project managers X.
> Project managers also Y ...
>
> contrast: Show differences between things.
> ... project X expanded.
> Project Y, though, shrunk ...
>
> emphasize: Restate a key idea in a different way.
> ... project X was delayed.
> As the schedule slipped ...
>
> expand: Show another aspect of an idea.
> ... causes project delays.
> Delays are not the only thing ...

Links: When a paragraph has related sentences, link them using words that guide the reader.

> compare: in comparison, in the same way, likewise, similarly
>
> contrast: although, however, in contrast, nevertheless, on the other hand, yet
>
> deduce: accordingly, as a result, consequently, hence, so, therefore, thus
>
> elaborate: after all, also, besides, for example, furthermore, in addition, moreover, specifically
>
> emphasize: above all, indeed, in fact, most important
>
> order: afterward, before, first, second, next, formerly, subsequently, then

Exercises

In both examples below, improve flow by doing the following:
- Begin the second paragraph with a transition sentence based on the underlined key word.
- Insert links at the beginning of sentences within the second paragraph.

Collection-type heritage <u>assets</u> acquired in fiscal 2000 amounted to $61 million. The public entrusts the government with them and holds it accountable for their preservation.

The Library of Congress holds the world's largest library collection: 115 million items. The Smithsonian Institution holds 140 million objects for public exhibition. The National Archives holds 2 million cubic feet of records, including the U.S. Constitution.

With a staff of 200 people from 30 countries, the United Nations University spends $36 million each year on research and policy studies by an international community of <u>scholars</u>. The University relies on them for advice and treats them as if they constituted an in-house think-tank.

The Governance Program produces recommendations for current political problems. The Environment Program focuses on sustainable management of natural resources. The Science Program studies the impact of new technologies on developing countries.

Solutions

Collection-type heritage assets acquired in fiscal 2000 amounted to $61 million. The public entrusts the government with them and holds it accountable for their preservation.

These assets are preserved in three places. First, the Library of Congress holds the world's largest library collection: 115 million items. **Second,** the Smithsonian Institution holds 140 million objects for public exhibition. **Third,** the National Archives holds 2 million cubic feet of records, including the U.S. Constitution.

With a staff of 200 people from 30 countries, the United Nations University spends $36 million each year on research and policy studies by an international community of scholars. The University relies on them for advice and treats them as if they constituted an in-house think-tank.

These scholars provide advice for a variety of programs. For example, the Governance Program produces recommendations for current political problems. **Also,** the Environment Program focuses on sustainable management of natural resources. **In addition,** the Science Program studies the impact of new technologies on developing countries.

INVITE

Wording matters, especially when we want not just to engage the reader, but to get the reader to respond, in the real-world sense. The response rate increases dramatically when we avoid putting road-blocks in front of our imperatives. Write directly to get results.

First version:

If you have any questions, you may contact me at any time.

Second version:

Contact me if you have any questions.

Now get rid of the "if" to create a final, brief, engaging version.

Final version:

Final version: Contact me with any questions.

VARIETY

Many people adopt a lifelong habit of writing most of their sentences in one preferred length and one preferred format. They might think such consistency makes them look capable or smart. But it's not about them—it's about the reader. Use variety to keep readers interested:

Length

Vary the length of your sentences. In most writing at work, sentences should be between 5 and 25 words long. If most of your sentences are about the same length, you should interject some variety, especially if the average length exceeds 20.

Format

Vary the format of your sentences: highlight important points at the beginning, middle, and end of your sentences.

> **Beginning:** To make a point, start with a prepositional phrase.
>
> **Middle:** Place words—between dashes—to interrupt and inform.
>
> **End:** Place an example after a colon: like this.

But, how to choose? Which sentences should we make long, and which short? In your writing at work, there's a general rule that's mostly common sense:

- Use long sentences when presenting a lot of information.
- Use short sentences when making important points.

Chapter 10 ~ Easy Reading

Exercise

Let's give this a try. Vary the sentences below:
- Start sentence 1 with a prepositional phrase.
- Condense sentence 2 down to a 5-word statement.
- Insert an interruption to highlight a strong point in sentence 3.
- Put an example word at the end of sentence 4.

We were able to find out what people thought about the cafeteria with a detailed survey. We tallied the results and discovered a trend in opinions of users that was not surprising. The menu was considered to be monotonous to the point of torture by every respondent. Cafeteria managers were finally able to learn that variety is the key to pleasing their customers.

Solution

> **With a detailed survey**, we were able to find out what people thought about the cafeteria.
>
> **The results were not surprising.**
>
> The menu was considered—**by every respondent**—to be monotonous to the point of torture.
>
> Cafeteria managers were finally able to learn the key to pleasing their customers: **variety**

Exercise

That was way too much fun. Let's try it again.
Vary the sentences below:
- Start sentence 1 with a prepositional phrase.
- End sentence 2 with a long phrase after a colon.
- Remove half the words (eleven of them) from sentence 4.

Some porcupines rapidly vibrate their tails when alarmed by a snake, producing a peculiar sound by the striking together of hollow quills. The attacker and the attacked use similar means to achieve the goal of making themselves as dreadful as possible to each other. Suppose those best able to frighten away their enemies escape, but those best fitted for killing and devouring survive in larger numbers. Then in the one case as in the other, the beneficial variations would commonly be preserved through the survival of the fittest.

Solution

> **When alarmed by a snake,** some porcupines rapidly vibrate their tails, producing a peculiar sound by the striking together of hollow quills.
>
> The attacker and the attacked use similar means **to achieve a common goal: making** themselves as dreadful as possible to each other.
>
> Suppose those best able to frighten away their enemies escape, but those best fitted for killing and devouring survive in larger numbers.
>
> **Then beneficial variations are preserved through survival of the fittest.**

METHODS OF ADDITION

There is another aspect of sentence variety that's worth thinking about: how we add information to a sentence. First of all, if we never added or combined information our sentences could be correct and informative, but rather dull:

> They ran the test twice. They did this for my benefit. The second test was unnecessary. The test itself is hopelessly flawed. The test does not measure BER performance of the transponder. The test does verify continuity of signal through the transponder. The contract requires that they test BER performance in the presence of noise. They placed the noise source downstream of the transponder. The proper test would place the noise source upstream of the transponder. Their resulting waterfall curve depicts the performance of the test equipment. The waterfall curve should depict the performance of the transponder. We should stop paying for their test. We should demand that they run our test correctly.

This is repetitive and a bit mind-numbing. It sounds like the facts one might record when assembling the knowledge base to be used in an expert system. But here's the thing: *you* are the expert. And you should be presenting information so that your readers get it without falling asleep.

How do we combine information into sentences in a way that doesn't bore the heck out of the reader? There are three ways:

- Attach
- Assign
- Accessorize

Attach

Use conjunctions to simply attach or connect things:

> They placed the noise source downstream of the transponder, **but** the proper test would place the noise source upstream.

We do this all the time, no big deal, right?

It is a big deal if that's all you do. The result would be:

They ran the test twice for my benefit, **but** the second test was unnecessary. The test itself is hopelessly flawed, **because** it does not measure BER performance of the transponder. The test does verify continuity of signal through the transponder, **even though** the contract requires that they test BER performance in the presence of noise. They placed the noise source downstream of the transponder, **but** he proper test would place the noise source upstream of the transponder. Their resulting waterfall curve depicts the performance of the test equipment, **while** the waterfall curve should depict the performance of the transponder. We should stop paying for their test, **or** we should demand that they run our test correctly.

This provides the reader with correct sentences and all the information. However, if people are forced to read another paragraph like that, and more besides, they might begin to feel oppressed by the incessant pounding of the one sentence form.

Assign

Here we take information and place it in a subordinate clause, which is a fancy way of saying make it report to and about a specific other thing: assign it to that thing. This is done with commas and a pronoun (*who, which, that*):

The test, which is hopelessly flawed, does not measure BER performance of the transponder.

Again, we have correct grammar and all the information. And it highlights an important point. But it's not a good thing to do in a majority of your sentences. Every instance is an interruption, however brief.

Accessorize

This is actually a loose version of an attach or an assign:

They placed the noise source downstream of the transponder, **the proper placement being upstream.**

Hopelessly flawed, the test does not measure BER performance of the transponder.

These are called free modifiers, where *free* means you are free to place the modifier anywhere: at the beginning, in the middle, or at the end of the sentence.

Elegant writing is usually created with a fair amount of accessorizing, some attaching, and a little bit of assigning.

Exercise

For the 13-sentence example we started with, accessorize, attach, and assign to make it lucid and maybe even elegant:

Solution

> For my benefit they ran the test twice, which was unnecessary. Their test, hopelessly flawed, does not measure BER performance of the transponder. It merely verifies continuity of signal through the transponder.
>
> The contract requires that they test BER performance in the presence of noise. They placed the noise source downstream of the transponder, the proper place being upstream. Their resulting waterfall curve depicts the performance of the test equipment, instead of the performance of the transponder. We should stop paying for their test, and we should demand that they run our test correctly.

This is very subjective stuff. But if you have progressed to the point of thoughtfully and carefully applying these techniques, you have surpassed the skills of most writing teachers. You are becoming a master at it yourself. Congrats!

FINAL COMMENTS

If you had to choose only one technique from this chapter, choose variety of sentence length. You have to keep the reader awake. It's that simple and that important. The act of editing sentences into differing lengths will help you make reader-oriented choices about grouping information and emphasizing important points. And the same editing efforts will naturally lead you to recognize other opportunities, including active voice, parallels, guides, and additions.

FAQs

Q: *I know I should avoid using the passive voice, but often I don't even recognize that I've used it! Is there anything I can do to either remind myself or spot it in my own writing?*

A: Step One is to train your mind to behave. When you edit your first draft use the Find function and search for three words: " was " " been " " by ". Include the space before and after each word. These three words are the most common parts of passive voice constructions. Step through each occurrence of each word and assess the need for a change to active voice. This should keep you busy with a sentence like: "The report was written by Amy, but should have been written by Ben." Step Two comes naturally. After you do Step One several times, you will begin to catch yourself as you start to write passive voice in the next thing you write. Step One is annoying but necessary. It's kind of like spritzing a kitten with water to make it learn not to do something.

Q: *I understand why I need to make my writing more engaging when my goal is to persuade or sell. Should I really use engaging language when I am writing more routine reports and messages?*

A: Yes, but let's explore what we mean by 'engage'. Our writing engages the reader on different levels:
   1. Keep the reader from falling asleep.
   2. Keep the reader from giving up.
   3. Make the reader comfortable.
   4. Make the reader interested.
   5. Convince the reader to agree.

Several of these levels are appropriate for routine writing at work. Persuading and selling use higher levels.

SECTION IV

Style & Format

People want to be comfortable with what they're reading, so we prepare our writing in familiar ways. This is a good thing. Do you think you would enjoy reading a report assembled by someone who is keen on redefining how reports should be structured? At work it helps to be predictable and consistent in how you write common documents. It puts people at ease.

Chapter 11: Document Style – A few guidelines will help you prepare properly-formatted announcements, letters, presentation charts, and your résumé. It may seem like common sense, but it's easy to lapse into bad document style.

Chapter 12: Email Style – Text on displays has replaced many of our telephone and face-to-face conversations. To use email well, you should practice with what to write, how to write it, and when to write it.

Chapter 13: Report Style – This subject could fill a book. But we'll focus on logical organization, document templates, topic order, and numbers in technical reports.

Chapter 14: Looking Good – How should you choose fonts? How much blank space is appropriate on a page? How can layout improve readability? All will be revealed.

~ *Subject in Action* ~

Nate wasn't a rebel. But he always bucked the system a little when it came to what he called "old fogey" rules, like dressing up for a wedding. When he landed his first job at a small company, he took this attitude with him. The management team and Nate's older coworkers were pretty cool. They didn't get upset with his casual emails and his edgy, even slightly irreverent, presentation style. They paid attention to his points and acknowledged his contributions.

Nate was happy with his success—until he realized that in the office he was often referred to as 'the kid.' He started to notice that although his ideas seemed to be accepted, his work was primarily focused on challenges internal to the company. His boss rarely assigned Nate important work that required interacting with people outside the office: customers, suppliers, and partners.

He recognized that his opportunity for advancement might be limited, so he raised his concerns with his boss. She was genuinely baffled. But a week later she called Nate back in for a follow-up conversation. She said she'd thought about what he had said and then she'd talked to a few people. She had come to realize that Nate's casual style of interaction with others had given everyone the impression that although Nate was a smart guy, he was probably not the kind of guy who would be serious about taking on more responsibility.

Furthermore, she realized that if he left that impression with her and others, it was likely he would do the same in critical external relationships. She said she wasn't demanding that Nate change but that he should be realistic and understand that maintaining his style would have an impact on his career growth.

CHAPTER 11

Document Style

> **In This Chapter**
>
> - Announce with purpose and focus.
> - Make letters consistent and assertive.
> - Presentation charts should be sparse.
> - Fill your résumé with action verbs.

WHY YOU SHOULD CARE

You will write a variety of documents at work. And each type of document requires a slightly different style. Yes, your prose should be correct, clear, and concise. But you also need to make decisions about:

- What to say.
- What to not say.
- How much of it to say.
- How to say it.

Of course, obvious, right? In concept, yes. But in practice, not so much. You should always be willing to put a little more effort into learning how to use your words appropriately to each writing situation, and document.

ANNOUNCEMENT

Are you new to the organization? Someone might say in your direction, "Hey, you're the newbie. We have to publish this announcement for everybody. Get the stuff and write the first draft." Lucky you, but don't despair. It's not too difficult.

The announcement is similar to a letter except that it is used to correspond with people inside the organization. It is used to inform or instruct. It used to be called a memo, and is now usually distributed via email.

Imagine your announcement will be posted on the wall at the entrance to the cafeteria. To entice people to read it as they walk by, follow these guidelines:

- **Tone:** Use a positive tone, especially in the subject line.
- **Subject:** Avoid acronyms, dates, and initials.
- **Reason:** Explicitly state the purpose of the announcement.
- **Parallels:** Present related statements in bulleted or numbered lists, ideally in brief imperatives.
- **Focus:** Deal only with the subject specified; that is, avoid introducing new topics.
- **Closing:** Tell the readers what you want them to do, even if this is just a restatement of the purpose.

Exercise

Follow the guidelines to improve this announcement:

To: All Employees	From: Don Chaffin
Subject: HR Summer 2012 Warning by D.C.	Date: May 6, 2012
Employees who spend more than three hours per day in front of a computer monitor may experience eye strain and headaches. This hazard can be avoided by taking three simple actions.	
Documents should be placed at the same distance from you as the monitor. Position the monitor perpendicular to and slightly below your line of sight. It helps to take a break every ten minutes, looking far away and making sure to blink.	
We in HR will publish the next summer warning, about lower back pain, in 2 weeks.	

Subject: _____

_____

- _____

- _____

- _____

_____

Don't you think your version would do a better job of enticing readers in line at the cafeteria? The best announcements—the ones most likely to be read—are concise, ideally not longer than one page.

Solution

Subject: **Protect Your Eyes**

The purpose of this announcement is to give you simple actions you can take to protect your eyes if you spend more than three hours per day in front of a computer monitor.

- **Place documents at the same distance from you as the monitor.**
- Position the monitor perpendicular to and slightly below your line of sight.
- **Take a break every ten minutes, looking far away and making sure to blink.**

Try these actions to avoid eye strain and headaches, and please suggest the same to your co-workers.

Exercise

You're on a roll! Try again:

To: Publications Staff	From: Martin Cutts
Subject: Bad Brochures and PDM Ignorance	Date: June 2, 2012

Recent brochures designed by our department have been difficult to read and in some cases simply ugly. Text has not been made easily accessible, mostly due to a lack of clear layout. The following are guidelines:

As a guide to legibility, one should use x-height. Set column width at 50-70 letters and spaces. Line spacing should be made to 1/5 of the type face. The temptation to fill whitespace with type should be resisted. Avoid single words forming the last line of a paragraph.

These and other guidelines from our Publications Design Manual were updated recently, but few people seem aware of that fact.

Subject: _____

_____

- _____

- _____

- _____

- _____

- _____

_____

Solution

Subject: **Good Brochure Layout**   [positive tone; no acronyms]

The purpose of this announcement is to improve the layout of text in our brochures by giving you the following guidelines: [state purpose]

- **Use x-height as your guide to legibility.** [text parallels]
- Set column width at 50-70 letters and spaces.
- **Make line spacing 1/5 of the type face.**
- **Resist the temptation to fill whitespace with type.**
- Avoid single words forming the last line of a paragraph.

Use these guidelines and others from our Publications Design Manual to make text more easily accessible to readers of our brochures. [no new topics; tell the readers what you want them to do]

LETTER

Don't waste your time memorizing rules of format for letters. Look them up when you need them. Instead, watch for the four areas where people most often go wrong in business letters:

Inconsistent Formality: The salutation and the complimentary closing should match: be informal with friends, be formal with strangers and organizations, and be consistent.

salutation		closing consistent with salutation	
Dear Bob:	informal	Kind regards,	Cheers,
Dear Mr. Rehme:			
Dear President:	↓	Sincerely yours,	Cordially,
Dear Board:			
Dear Academy:	formal	Yours truly,	Respectfully,

Ponderous references: Avoid phrases like *above-mentioned* or *aforementioned*. It is unnecessary and puts the reader to sleep. Also, you can always find a better way to say *with reference to*.

Half thoughts: Use complete sentences, even when stating the subject of the letter. It will be read by a human, not a computer.

Weak suggestions: Most business letters should end with a call to action. Make it assertive and specific.

Exercise

In the letter below, find examples of the four problem areas and suggest improvements.

Dear Academy:

With reference to the movie, *Evolution*, directed by Ivan Reitman. Please ensure that the Academy gives careful consideration to the aforementioned movie. Despite the unabashed product placement, it is a well-acted romantic action comedy. I hope you get a chance to view the movie by the end of the year.

Kind Regards,

Note: Business letters are changing. The word *Dear* in a salutation has become optional. In many organizations, the salutation and complimentary closing are both no longer used. Below the salutation, or in place of it, a subject line has become an acceptable part of the business letter.

Solution

Dear Academy:
I am writing about the movie, *Evolution*, directed by Ivan Reitman. Please ensure that the Academy gives careful consideration to **the movie**. Despite the unabashed product placement, it is a well-acted romantic action comedy.
I will deliver a DVD of the movie to your office on 12 December. Respectfully,

PRESENTATION

Use these guidelines to fix the presentation chart below:

Headline: Ideally, write a subject with no verbs. If you must write a sentence, keep it brief and use active voice.

Bullets: Use parallel construction at each level. Put main point first, then supporting data. Never write a whole paragraph.

Fonts: Consistently use a limited set, never smaller than 12pt.

Graphic: Support the headline. Match the text. Choose well:

what you want to show	which to use
contribution of components	
differences among items	
change over time	
distribution of occurrence	
correlation between variables	

Exercise

The highest proportion of revenues was generated by Project B. Changes among projects were as expected.

- It is expected that Project A will soon expire. This will free up staff for other projects.
- **Project B doubled in size to produce 60% of revenues.**
- Project C contribution remained at 30% of revenues.
- Generation of revenues continues to change among projects.

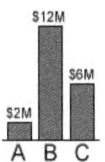

$12M, $6M, $2M
A B C

Solution

Project Revenues

- Project B doubled to produce 60% of revenues.

- Project C remained level at 30% of revenues.

- Project A provided 10% of revenues but expires soon.

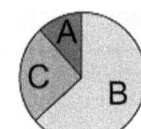

Seems to say less? That's the point. You will be saying what needs to be said.

Exercise

This is important stuff. You should practice more. Edit the heck out of this one. This time, you'll have some space to work.

> **Applications continue to be received. The highest number of applications was received in the third quarter of the year.**
>
> - Applications are tracked and reviewed by senior staff.
> - **Of the Q3 applications, 40% had unacceptable qualifications.**
> - The normal quarterly rate of apps was seen to increase from 24 last year to about 28 this year. (This is most likely due to our increased advertising in the newspaper.)
> - Applications are typically even through all four quarters. For the past decade this has been the case. Our surprising Q3 result, twice the normal rate, has yet to be explained.

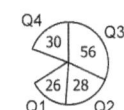

Solution

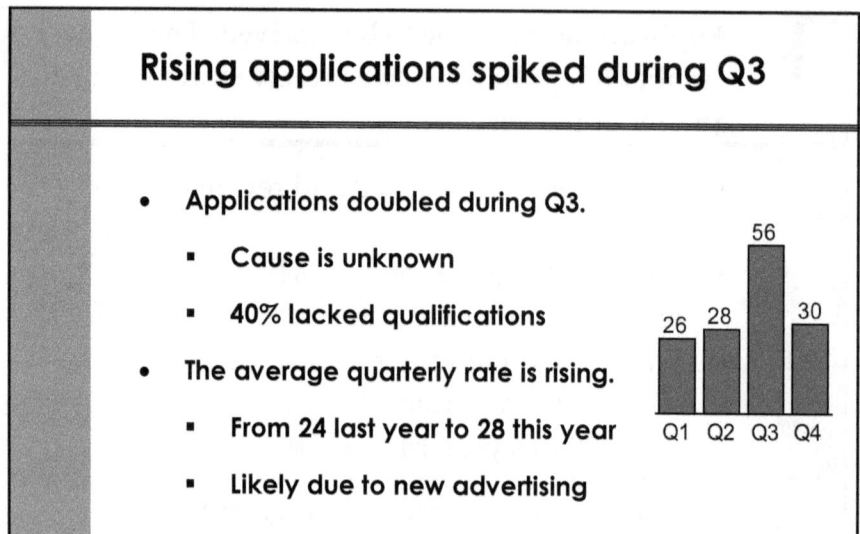

RÉSUMÉ

Employers need to quickly answer two questions: Might the person represented by this résumé match our needs? Should I pass this résumé on to someone else in the company? Your job is to write your résumé so that they answer, "Yes!"
Here are six rules to make that happen.

1. Use action verbs. The résumé is the worst place to use weak verbs or passive voice.

> weak verb and passive voice: Training seminars were put together for clear writing.
>
> action verb and active voice: I organized seminars to train people to write clearly.

2. Use incomplete sentences. The subject, I (that is, you), is always implied.

> complete: I organized seminars to train people to write clearly.
>
> preferred: Organized seminars to train people to write clearly.

3. Use the good stuff. Include only entries that highlight a capability or an accomplishment.

> bland stuff: The company offered the negotiations seminar to new managers.
>
> good stuff: Developed a negotiations seminar for new managers.

4. Avoid spelling errors. One error justifies throwing your résumé in the garbage can.

5. Avoid pompous fluff. Consider the following text:

> Self-motivated, hands-on team player with a proven track record in adding value.

Now answer the question: Would *you* keep reading this fluff?

6. Avoid irrelevant data. Personal data (gender, age, race, health, marital status) can cause legal problems for employers; don't include it. Also omit social security number, salaries, and irrelevant associations.

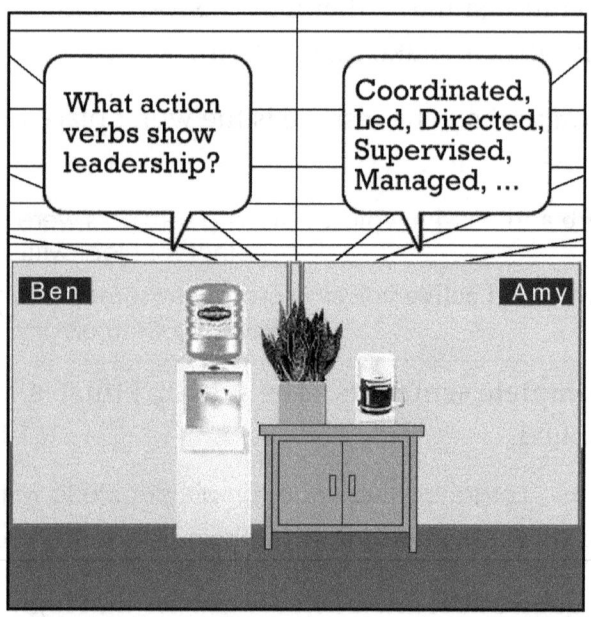

Here are a few more issues to consider for your résumé:

Length: One page is ideal, especially with fewer than 5 years of work experience. Never more than 2 pages.

Scanning: Make your résumé scanner friendly: Left justify the entire document. Use a sans-serif font, size 10 or higher. Avoid italics, underlining, parentheses, brackets, graphics, and lines.

Internet: Create a text version of your résumé to submit via email or webpage. Make it computer friendly: avoid tabs and unnecessary hard returns. To get flagged by filters, use keywords more than you would on a paper résumé.

Exercise

Follow the six rules to make this résumé shine:

Name
Address . Phone . Email

EXPERIENCE

Training Coordinator, St. Mary's College, San Antonio, Texas 2006 - present
- Enrolled employees in training classes and prepared facilities for presentations.
- A new class in conflict resolution was set up for department administrators.
- Employee participation in training classes varied with staff size.

Assistant Manager, Barnes & Noble Bookstore, San Antonio, Texas 2002 - 2006
- I managed inventory for books, music CDs, calendars, and magazines.
- Lead book discussion groups and arranged author events.

EDUCATION

Diploma, San Houston High School, San Antonio, Texas 2002

ACTIVITIES

Train tutors for Literacy Volunteers
Religious Advisor, Hash House Harriers of San Antonio

Note: These exercises are for chronological résumés. Refer to *The Gregg Reference Manual* for other types of résumés.

Solution

Name
Address . Phone . Email

EXPERIENCE

Training Coordinator, St. Mary's College, San Antonio, Texas 2006 - present
- Enrolled employees in training classes and prepared facilities for presentations.
- **Developed** a new class in conflict resolution ~~was set up~~ for department administrators.
        [action verb]
- ~~Employee participation in training classes varied with staff size.~~
        [not a capability or accomplishment]

Assistant Manager, Barnes & Noble Bookstore, San Antonio, Texas 2002 - 2006
- **Managed** inventory for books, music CDs, calendars, and magazines.
        [incomplete sentence preferred]
- **Led** book discussion groups and arranged author events. [spelling]

EDUCATION

Diploma, San Houston High School, San Antonio, Texas 2002

ACTIVITIES

Train tutors for Literacy Volunteers
~~Religious Advisor, Hash House Harriers of San Antonio~~
        [irrelevant association]

Exercise

Try another one:

Name

Address . Phone . Email

EXPERIENCE

Humen Resources Director, Thomson-Shore, Dexter, Michigan 2004 to present
- I managed a staff of 15 and reported progress to VP of operations at weekly meetings.
- Coordinated staff needs including recruiting, training, benefits, and compensation.
- Acheived a company goal of reducing the cost of our insurance plans by 25%.
- Approved salary plans and established employee awards program.

Benefits Administrator, Central Michigan Paper Company, Ada, Michigan 2000 - 2004
- Lead a company-wide review and upgrade of software for benefits management.
- Negotiated contracts for HMOs, PPOs, and life insurance carriers.
- Instrumental in championing process improvements to add value to the company's bottom line.

Human Resources Associate, MeadWestvaco Papers, Escanaba, Michigan 1994 - 1998
- Orientation presentations were put together and given to new hires.
- Completed a company rotation program, with 4-month assignments in payroll, accounting, recruiting, marketing, sales, and purchasing.
- The company grew from 950 to 1250 employees during my tenure.

EDUCATION

BS Psychology, Northern Michigan University 1994

MBA, Human Resources emphasis, University of Michigan 2000

ACTIVITIES

Chairperson, Professional Emphasis Group in Technology, Society for Human Resources Management

Co-Author: IT Systems for Benefits Administration, 2005, McGraw-Hill

Solution

Name
Address . Phone . Email

EXPERIENCE

Human Resources Director, Thomson-Shore, Dexter, Michigan 2004 to present   [spelling]

- **Managed** a staff of 15 and reported progress to VP of operations at weekly meetings.
    [incomplete sentence preferred]
- Coordinated staff needs including recruiting, training, benefits, and compensation.
- **Achieved** a company goal of reducing the cost of our insurance plans by 25%.   [spelling]
- Approved salary plans and established employee awards program.

Benefits Administrator, Central Michigan Paper Company, Ada, Michigan 2000 - 2004

- **Led** a company-wide review and upgrade of software for benefits management.   [spelling]
- Negotiated contracts for HMOs, PPOs, and life insurance carriers.
- **Saved the company $150K per year by improving enrollment processes.**   [accomplishment]

Human Resources Associate, MeadWestvaco Papers, Escanaba, Michigan 1994 - 1998

- **Developed and presented** orientations for new hires.
    [action verbs in active voice]
- Completed a company rotation program, with 4-month assignments in payroll, accounting, recruiting, marketing, sales, and purchasing.
- ~~The company grew from 950 to 1250 employees during my tenure.~~   [not a capability or accomplishment]

EDUCATION

MBA, Human Resources emphasis, University of Michigan 2000
BS Psychology, Northern Michigan University 1994
[reverse chronological order in EDUCATION and EXPERIENCE sections]

ACTIVITIES

Chairperson, Professional Emphasis Group in Technology, Society for Human Resources Management

Co-Author: IT Systems for Benefits Administration, 2005, McGraw-Hill

FINAL COMMENTS

At this point, you know more about appropriate writing style for announcements, letters, presentation charts, and résumés than more than half of your peers. Seriously. A surprising number of young professionals consider their writing 'adequate enough' to get any job done. They have yet to learn: part of the job is to communicate to others *in their preferred format* what was done *and* why it matters *and* what should be done next *and* who should do it, etc.

Some companies have a Style Guide for writing. If your employer has one, and coworkers take it seriously, be sure to read it. Sometimes these guides are for marketing people so that they present words, brands, or corporate statements a certain way. Often, however, these guides are prepared as thorough references for showing people both writing styles and preferred formats for announcements, letters, presentation charts, and other documents.

Even if your employer has a writing guide, if your boss prefers things done a certain way, go with the flow. Use documents your boss has prepared or approved as templates for the things you must write.

FAQs

Q: *In a letter, is the phrase "To Whom It May Concern" acceptable?*

A: Yes, if you are writing an open reference letter, or if you are putting the letter in a bottle to be cast into the sea. Otherwise, use the name of the organization (for example, *Dear Academy:*).

Q: *How do I decide which document style is best for what I'm doing? I never know when to write an email versus a letter.*

A: First of all, it is assumed here that you are asking about one-to-many correspondence. Honestly, your employer sets the stage for this issue. Some companies are committed to saving trees and hence avoid paper correspondence whenever possible.

One thing to keep in mind is the ease with which emails can be re-distributed. If you would prefer that your message not be widely disseminated, especially outside the company, use hardcopy.

Another concern is the need for a group of people to remember to do something days or weeks in the future. A paper announcement functions in this case as a physical and constant reminder. An email doesn't help as much, being represented by a few words on a subject line that gets bumped farther down the Inbox list all week long.

Another topic is email versus letter, in one-to-one correspondence. In most cases, emails have replaced letters. However, a letter should be used if you are writing something that is confidential or formal. A letter with company letterhead represents and commands respect. Most emails are viewed as informal notes sent in haste. And old emails (always saved somewhere by your employer) are too easily found and exploited by hackers and attorneys.

CHAPTER 12

Email Style

> **In This Chapter**
>
> - Always write the message first.
> - Use contractions as your default style.
> - Extra care can fine tune the tone.
> - Make subject lines interesting to read.

WHY YOU SHOULD CARE

At work, we typically write our emails in a hurry. This can result in messages that confuse or offend the reader. It can also result in mistakes that make us look really bad, such as a misspelled word in an important email to an important person.

A few guidelines will keep your emails on target and keep you out of trouble. Please take this seriously. Bad habits in using email can jeopardize your job or ruin your career. It does happen. Google it. Then sit back and ask yourself: all that school, all that interviewing, just to get this job—do I want to chance blowing it all on a careless mistake in an email?

HOW TO WRITE EMAILS

(1) First write the Message: (type it, then edit, then edit again)

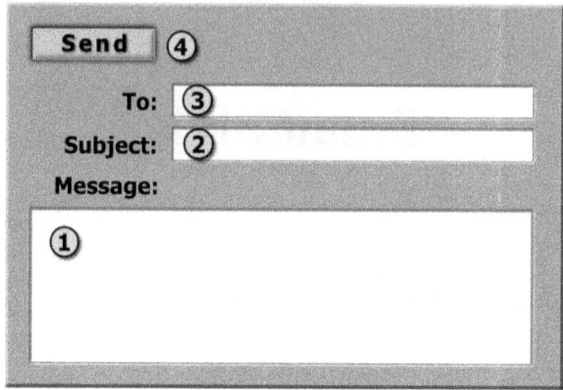

(2) Second, write the Subject.

(3) Wait until you are satisfied with *both* of these before you type the email address of the recipient.

By adopting this simple habit, you will avoid sending an email before it's polished. Writing in this order, you are:
- more relaxed when you write the message,
- better prepared to write a good subject, and
- less likely to inadvertently send an incomplete message.

Message: Opening & Closing

The safest default strategy for the Opening and Closing is to echo what you are already getting from that person. If you are initiating an exchange, the Opening and the Closing perform important functions:
- They show how you view the nature of your relationship with the recipient.
- They show how you wish to be addressed.

In your Opening, try to avoid barking out a name; it never hurts to be gracious and start with the word Dear. Use punctuation to show how formal you want to be.

Dear Ms. Diaz:	suitable for someone you don't know
Dear Cameron,	acceptable for an acquaintance
Cameron,	typical for friends and colleagues

The following are common and acceptable in your Closing:

| Sincerely, Leslie | Best regards, Jesse | Regards, Alex | Best, Pat |

A blank Opening and Closing is acceptable if your email is part of an ongoing conversation with a peer.

Message: request etiquette

It's easy to send emails, so it's easy to make requests. Self-control is essential to avoiding indiscriminate and poorly-worded requests. A short checklist can help.

☐ I really need this.
- The reader is not imposed upon to do unnecessary work.

☐ I am asking for only one thing.
- The reader has a message that is easy to answer and file.

☐ I am asking early in the email.
- The reader doesn't have to read carefully all the way to the end.

☐ I am asking in a single-sentence paragraph.
- The reader quickly recognizes the request.

☐ I am brief but specific.
- The reader quickly gets what I want.

Message: response etiquette

People expect fast responses to their email requests, while you get more and more email every day. A short checklist can keep you out of trouble.

☐ I reply quickly, if only to schedule a response.
- The reader is not kept in the dark.

☐ I answer at the top.
- The reader is not annoyed by having to scroll down.

☐ I respond in kind: chatty or terse.
- The reader feels comfortable with our communication.

☐ I acknowledge and explain atypical brevity.
- The reader is not offended by an abrupt reply.
  example Closings:
    On the run,   More to follow,

☐ I apologize if I was late; I am self-deprecating.
- The reader won't hold a grudge.
  example Closing:
    A thousand apologies for being so late,

Message: tricky nice words

Polite words are polite when spoken politely. In an email, they can backfire through no fault of your own. A recipient in a bad mood can infer a tone you never intended.

Risky	◀ Tone	Safe
Would you please remember to call me tomorrow?	◀ obnoxious	Please call me tomorrow.
Thank you for making sure I get the report.	◀ snotty	I appreciate your help in getting the report to me.

Message: contractions

Avoid sounding like a scolding parent. Use contractions as your default style.

Risky	◀ Tone	Safe
I do not want to plan another meeting.	◀ fussy	I don't want to plan another meeting.
I am surprised you did not call.	◀ judgmental	I'm surprised you didn't call.

Message: typing

Spelling and grammar should be as in a letter—correct. And anyone who writes an email like this:

> hi - i heard u r done - plz send it ok? regds

is also saying, "you are not worth the effort for me to be professional and type using standard conventions."

Message: punctuation

Punctuation was created to mark separate thoughts and to guide the reading of bad handwriting. With text on computer screens, proper punctuation is not as necessary as it used to be. Adjust your punctuation to your situation.

Your situation	Your punctuation
The recipient is senior to you.	Make it correct.
You are replying to an email that was written with correct punctuation.	Make it correct.
Meaning could be drastically altered. No Thanks to you, X happened. [oops!] No. Thanks to you, X happened. [okay]	Make it correct.
The recipient is a friend.	Okay, relax —
You are both texting.	u can chill dude

Message: paragraphs

A few rules go a long way. Give the reader:

- Short paragraphs.
- Space between paragraphs.
- Separate paragraphs for separate topics.
- Key points at the beginning of each paragraph.

The Subject Line

A good Subject Line entices people to open your email. A generic Subject Line is an invitation to delay or delete. Here are some rules that can help:

	Subject Lines	
Rule	**Bad**	**Good**
Avoid looking like spam.	Quick question	Cancel our telecon?
Say something informative.	Important	Auditors arriving soon
Indicate all important topics.	Agenda	Agenda & change of venue
Include relevant names.	Meeting	Addison's meeting

Above all: use it to succinctly summarize your message and to hook your reader. We all get too much email, so we all delete a lot of email based on what we see in the Subject Line.

Example

Jordan Botha and Taylor Lee work at Waihonu Swimwear. Jordan recently joined the company as a manager in the Sales Department. Taylor has been with the company for many years and is a manager in the Personnel Department. Taylor hosted the day-long orientation for new hires. It was at this meeting that Taylor and Jordan met for the first time. After that, they met briefly one other time in the company cafeteria.

Jordan wrote the following email to send to Taylor:

To:

From: Jordan Botha <jordanb@waihonu.com>

Subject: orientation

Message: Hello,

At the new-hire orientation meeting last week, you said we must decide about signing up our families for a medical plan by the end of the month, otherwise they would not be covered until next year. You also said I would receive that pamphlet for the credit union as soon as it was available. I have not received any pamphlet, and I am curious when it will be delivered. I made my decision about which plan I want to sign up for. When should I stop by to sign the papers? As you could guess, my workday is rather full with all the new people and procedures to get used to, so it may take some doing to find a match in our schedules. Thanks for making sure I get the papers signed. I look forward to your response.

Sincerely,

Jordan Botha

Let's re-write the email for Jordan. We can make up any details, especially about the plan or the pamphlet.

Here is what we do:
- Decide what topics are important and what topics could be ignored.
- Break things up into brief paragraphs.
- Choose appropriate words for the Opening and Closing.
- Check grammar and spelling.
- Write a compelling Subject Line.
- Fill in the email address.

Here is a result:

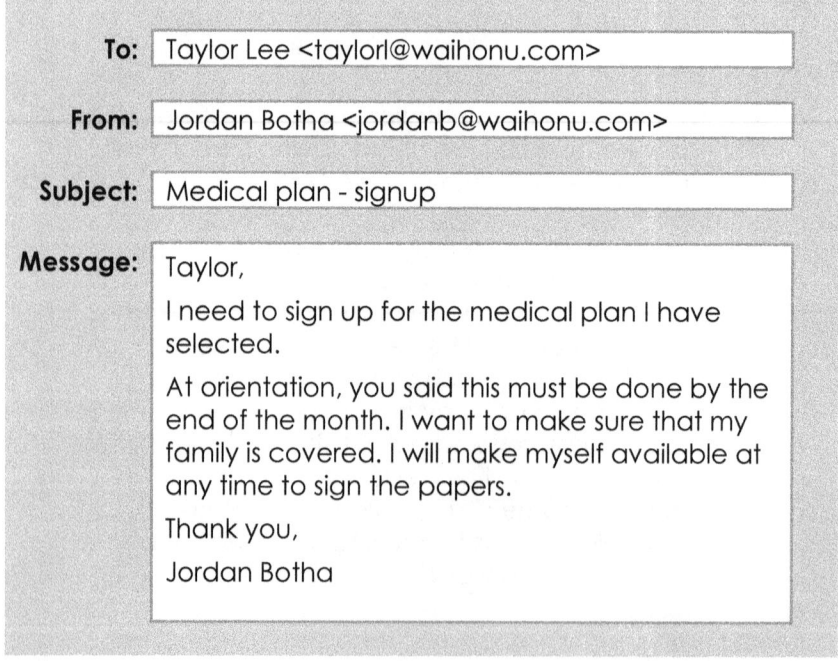

Exercise

Now pretend you are Taylor. You are remiss: you forgot about Jordan's email, and now the end of the month has passed. You will take responsibility for fixing things. Compose your response email. Make up any details.

To:	
From:	Taylor Lee <taylorl@waihonu.com>
Subject:	
Message:	

Solution

(one example)

To:	Jordan Botha <jordanb@waihonu.com>
From:	Taylor Lee <taylorl@waihonu.com>
Subject:	RE: Medical plan - signup
Message:	Jordan,
	I will make sure you and your family are covered.
	An exception will be made for our being outside the signup window. Stop by the Personnel office to sign the papers - at any time.
	I am terribly sorry for being so late in responding.
	Sincere apologies,
	Taylor Lee

FINAL COMMENTS

All it takes is one email booboo to permanently tarnish your reputation. Avoid this by adopting a few habits in an email regimen:

- Take your time: wait to enter the To: email; type your message first, then edit it, then look it over again.
- Take your time: adjust formality and tone for the reader, and go overboard with politeness and self-deprecation.
- Take your time: write a subject line that is so engaging people will marvel at it and tell their friends and family.

Take your time? Are you crazy, man? I'm busy at work. I don't have time to spend perfecting the things I type in my emails.

Yes, you do. The time referred to here is in minutes, not hours. And the regimen you develop will turn those minutes into seconds for emails you write in the future, when you're so good at it, it'll scare you.

FAQs

Q: *My boss gets mad at me because I leave the subject line blank. What's her problem?*

A: Imagine yourself as a youngster. You're in the kitchen snacking on warm pie topped with ice cream. Your little brother shouts from upstairs, "Hey! Come up here!" You shout, "Why?" and take another bite of the delicious dessert before all the ice cream melts. Your brother screams, *"Because!* Just come *up* here!"

When you send your boss an email with no subject line, you're behaving like the annoying little brother. Sorry to bring your imaginary family into this.

Q: *Is it OK to use emoticons in my emails?*

A: Yes, but only in emails that are the equivalent of casual conversations. Serious conversations deserve serious emails. And then there's the height of seriousness: legal troubles. An attorney could mislead a jury into believing your emoticon in a critical email was meant in a way you didn't intend. No way, right? Way. Your emails belong to your employer, not to you. If your employer is investigated, or gets sued, or sues someone, the company emails get trotted out in court for all to see.

Q: *Sometimes I have a lot to say so I send long emails. My peers say they don't bother to read long emails. How else can I get important information across?*

A: You're not writing emails. You're emailing reports. And you're probably overinflating the importance of some of the information. Put the information in a document, attach it to the email, and then do two things:
 1. Write a brief message with statements that engage the reader and that explain what is in the attachment.
 2. Write a subject line that the reader will have no trouble finding weeks from now.

CHAPTER 13

Report Style

> **In This Chapter**
>
> - Group ideas in a logical hierarchy.
> - The status report: answer questions.
> - Write summaries last, but place first.
> - Guidelines help with writing numbers.

WHY YOU SHOULD CARE

You gained a lot of knowledge in school. Now you're applying that knowledge and reporting your results. All that effort comes to naught if your words cause readers to frown in confusion or fall asleep from boredom.

Reports are as formal as it gets at work. Reports are to tuxedos as emails are to jeans. Sort of. It's serious communications, often because it represents an official position or it meets a contractual requirement. Important people are likely to read it, serious people you don't want to disappoint. The most scrutiny you will get at work for your writing will be for a report.

PYRAMID LOGIC

The biggest problem with reports has little to do with grammar or clarity. The biggest problem is bad structure due to a lack of early thinking and planning. Yes, outlining. But outlining does not have to be drudgery. It can be fun, and it can even make the actual writing much easier.

Another approach is to outline visually with a pyramid and a strict logical associations of ideas. This looks simple, but is extremely analytical.

It has only three rules:

Ideas: Use ideas, not topics, and write them as brief assertive sentences.

Pyramid: Arrange your ideas in a pyramid, topped by your main idea.

Unity: Rewrite each idea so that it summarizes the ideas below it and links to the idea beside it.

Example:

	To win more contracts we need more training in writing skills.	
	↓ summarize	
We lost several contracts because our proposals were written poorly.	→ link	Our writers are sure that a course in writing skills will improve our proposals.

Easy peasy, right? Maybe, maybe not. With every level the complexity increases dramatically. But if you can get all your flash cards to line up right, you'll have a rock-solid report.

Exercise

Identify which two ideas should be switched.

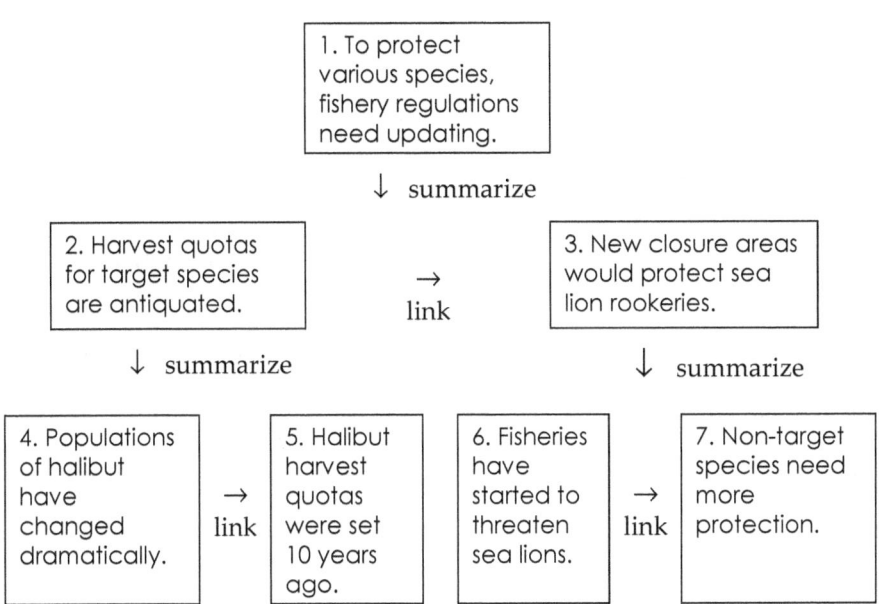

Note: The pyramid outline is more suited to reports written to persuade than it is suited to reports written merely to inform.

Solution

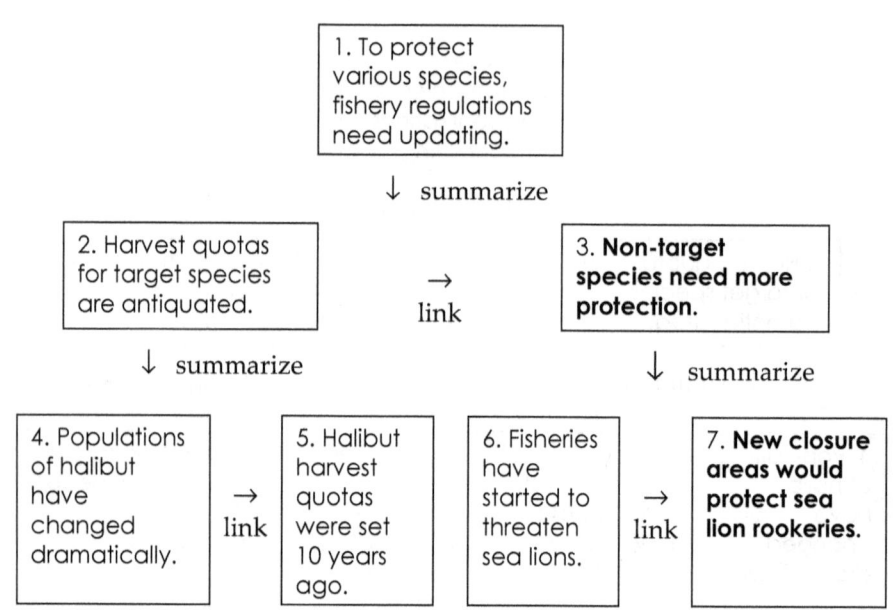

The benefits of using a pyramid to outline include:
1. The main idea will be clear to you and the reader.
2. The rewriting of linked ideas improves logical flow.
3. The juggling of ideas enhances creativity.
4. Section headings will jump out at you.
5. Writing can commence anywhere.

STATUS REPORT

The writing of reports is a large topic. Let's narrow it down a bit and focus on the most common report: the status report. We'll concentrate on the subtle but significant challenges people face when writing reports at work:

- Getting past the anxiety of having to write a report.
    - (fear of high school essays)
- Getting started writing anything at all.
    - (writer's block)
- Getting locked into a non-optimal framework.
    - (anchoring on first thoughts)
- Not considering how the reader might react.
    - (assuming we're all on the same page)

To deal with these challenges, start by saying to yourself:

"I'm not writing a report, I'm just filling in a *template*. I'll write the summary *last*. And when I'm writing that summary, I'll divine with my crystal ball what the reader will *think* and *feel* and *do* when reading that summary."

Status reports are typically written for fellow employees. Most of these reports can be based on this generic template:

template	stuff to write
Background	Introduce people and the problem.
Facts	Present details about what happened.
Outcome	Describe results and effects.
Summary	Summarize the main point.

Switch it up

If you write the summary first, you might write more of an introduction than a summary. If you write the summary last, you are working with a better awareness of your material, and you are more likely to have a better understanding of what are the most important points to make.

The summary is for the benefit of key decision makers. These people are very busy. They will read the summary carefully and might only skim the rest of the report.

Make that summary a true summary, not a first-draft introduction.

Then, when you are done with your first draft, place the summary in its proper position: right up front for the busy reader who wants to decide what to do about this fantastic report you wrote.

report

Summary

Background

Facts

Outcome

Questions to answer

For your first draft, start by answering relevant questions:

Trip report:

template	stuff to write: answers to questions

Background	Introduce people and the problem.
	  Who went where?
	  Why and when?

Facts	Present details about what happened.
	  What work did you do?
	  What didn't go right?
	  What did you do about it?

Outcome	Describe results and effects.
	  Is the work all done?
	  What still needs to be done?

Summary	Summarize the main point. What did you achieve that the reader most wants to know about?

Inspection report:

template	stuff to write: answers to questions

Background	Introduce people and the problem.
	  What was inspected and why?
	  Who inspected? Where and when?

Facts	Present details about what happened.
	  How many things were inspected?
	  What were their conditions?
	  What conditions need to be fixed?
	  How much work needs to be done?

Outcome	Describe results and effects.
	  What were the general results?
	  What are the recommendations?

Summary	Summarize the main point. What are the main results that the reader most wants to know?

Progress report:

template	stuff to write: answers to questions
Background	Introduce people and the problem. 　What is the motivator for recent efforts?
Facts	Present details about what happened. 　What work has been done? 　What problems were encountered? 　How did the problems affect progress? 　What is being done now?
Outcome	Describe results and effects. 　What will be done next? 　When will it be done?
Summary	Summarize the main point. 　What about the overall situation does the reader most want to know?

Project completion report:

template	stuff to write: answers to questions
Background	Introduce people and the problem. 　What was the purpose? 　Were schedules and budgets met? 　Who was involved?
Facts	Present details about what happened. 　What did we accomplish? 　What problems arose? 　How did we solve them? 　What varied from the plan? 　Why? And what will that change?
Outcome	Describe results and effects. 　What's interesting about the outcome? 　What follow-up action is needed?
Summary	Summarize the main point. 　What about the project does the reader most want to know?

Exercise

Imagine you are a high-ranking engineer at SpaceTech in Los Angeles. You provide technical advice to a variety of Program Offices at the Air Force's Space Systems Center. At the request of the Integrated Defense Links Program Office, you recently visited Robard Aerospace, a contractor that builds satellites. You were asked by several people to write reports:

1. Major Donald Nelson wants a progress report on the preparation of satellite 8-4 for transport.

2. Chief Engineer John O'Donnell wants a trip report on all that happened, including testing of satellite 9-1.

Start by reading over the notes you made on your trip:

2012-08-11 – Shuttle bus crowded again. Long lines at LAX security. We travel too much. SJ: got a Mustang at Avis. Fun cruise up 101 with the top down. Blue Cube is no more. 9:20am. Robard security went smooth this time. Met up with Gil Waxman. He's still slicing the ball despite my advice. Spent most of the morning in the test control bay. 10:00am. Inspected satellite #8.4 for residue from spray painting of walls in bay 3 while HVAC ductwork was not isolated. Gil rather quiet, with good reason. How do you explain an oops like this when you're building $300M satellites? And they should have told us earlier. Residue undetectable on surfaces and thermal blankets. Solar arrays had not yet been installed. 10:45am. Disconnected test cables. Verified capping of connectors. 11:45am. Lunch at Charlie's Café. 1:00pm. Final charge/top-off, of batteries. Detected 40 mA draw; isolated to command receiver 2. Reconnected test cable to power it down. Disconnected and verified proper capping. Verified nominal trace current. 2:15pm. Shipment chassis arrived. Witnessed, signed, for final stow and lockdown of payload antennas. 4:00pm. Gil left for tournament play. In the test lab offices, talked to other engineers from SpaceTech who are up reviewing test data for #9.1. John Roberson signing off on command subsystem. Jonathan Davis signing off on *payload T2; he's checking their BER test. We went to Maria Elena's for dinner. Dragged them to Los Gatos for Full Spectrum Jazz. Enjoyed the Belgian White Ale. Back to Courtyard.*

2012-08-12 – 8:30am. Gil on edge; he didn't break 90. Satellite #8.4 – final expansion and retraction of solar arrays. Had to stop twice: resonant vibrations. Verified with Melodee, MRC, back in A9, that magnitudes and frequencies were acceptable. Recorded the event, but signed off on procedure. 10:15am. Rolled satellite to outer bay. Placed on the shipping chassis. Crane certified, operated smoothly. 12:15pm. Lunchbreak - trim at Professional Cuts. Diana gushing about the grandkids. Tom is a busy boy. 1:00pm. Enclosed 8.4 with transport faring. Perfect fit all around. Witnessed and signed status sheet for sealing of faring. Gil showed me the transport plan and schedule for shipping the bird to Vandenberg. All per contract. 2:30pm. Satellite #9.1. Read test results and signed off on payload T4 tests except the BER. Looked for the T4 engineers. Conveniently missing. Changed return flight to last one, at 11pm, just in case. 4:30pm. Finally talked with engineers. Verified they did wire the BER test as shown on the diagram. They are obstinately clueless about the test being done bass-ackwards. The test is little more than a signal continuity check, which is accomplished in four of the other tests. The noise source must be upstream of the transponder to test the BER performance. Communications 101. Couldn't convince them. Used car salesmen. I refused to sign-off on BER test. And told them that Major Nelson now shares my concern. 5:30pm. Gil brought me over to their supervisor, who claimed enough interest to look into it. Agitated by my refusal to sign. Good. He threatened that it would delay the contract. I said it would make the program shorter and less expensive if we deleted unnecessary testing from the cost-plus contract. Smiled. Nodded. Left. 6:15pm. Keplers, got a new Haldeman novel for Teri. Mexican Lasagne at Café Borrone. 7:00pm. Menlo Park. Dan's quintet at the church. Warm, sparkling SV night drive back to SJ.

Write the first draft of your **progress report**, using a few sentences to answer the questions.

Background: What is the motivator for recent efforts?

Facts: What work has been done? What problems were encountered? How did the problems affect progress? What is being done now?

Outcome: What will be done next? When will it be done?

Summary: What about the overall situation does the reader most want to know?

Solution

Progress Report (a second draft, or so)

SPACETECH   200 North Douglas St, El Segundo, CA 90245

Date: August 14, 2012
From: Joe Judge, Principal Engineer,
Systems Engineering Group
To: Major Nelson
Integrated Defense Links Program Office
Subject: Progress on IDLSat Block 8-4

All final checks on Block 8-4 were nominal. The satellite is ready for transport to Vandenberg AFB.

[summary]

I visited the Robard facility in Sunnyvale on August 11-12. At the request of the Program Office, I was to inspect the satellite and witness packaging for transport.

[background]

We carefully searched for spray paint contamination, but found no residue on the surfaces or the thermal blankets. I witnessed and signed off on the stowing of antennae, retraction of the solar arrays, mating to the shipping chassis, and sealing of the transport faring.

[work done]

After battery final charge, we detected a 40 mA draw. Command receiver 2 was shut down, and we verified nominal trace current. While retracting solar arrays, twice experienced resonant vibrations, which were deemed acceptable by Melodee Lydon, MRC.

[problems encountered]

With your concurrence, the contractor is authorized to ship Block 8-4. Test progress on Block 9-1 is nominal. However, the Program Office should consider cancelling the improper BER test on T4.

[outcome]

Chapter 13 ~ Report Style 219

Write the first draft of your **trip report**, using a few sentences to answer the questions.

> Background: Who went where? Why and when?
>
>
>
> Facts: What work did you do? What didn't go right? What did you do about it?
>
>
>
> Outcome: Is the work all done? What still needs to be done?
>
>
>
> Summary: What did you achieve that the reader most wants to know about?

Solution

Trip Report (a second draft, or so)

SPACETECH   200 North Douglas St, El Segundo, CA 90245

Date: August 14, 2012
From: Joe Judge, Principal Engineer,
             Systems Engineering Group
To: John O'Donnell, Chief Engineer,
             Integrated Defense Links Program Office
Subject: Trip to Robard

Progress is satisfactory for the IDLSat program at Robard, except for the flawed testing of BER on certain payloads.

[summary]

I visited the Robard facility in Sunnyvale on August 11-12. Part of the second day was spent locating and consulting with engineers about the BER test on payload T4.

[background]

I observed and approved the stowing of appendages and the packaging of IDLSat 8-4. I reviewed communications test data for IDLSat 9-1, with no new problems found. I verified that the BER test on payload T4 was incorrectly configured.

[work done]

I unfortunately could not convince the payload engineers that their BER test is not a BER test of the hardware. I recommended to Major Nelson that this test no longer be run; it's little more than a continuity check and is therefore an unnecessary expense. I also recommended that the same issue be investigated for payload T2.

[problems encountered]

In short: the contractor is authorized to ship IDLSat 8-4; progress on IDLSat 9-1 is on schedule; and, some of the contractor payload engineers need to take a refresher course in communication systems.

[outcome]

HOW SHOULD I SHOW NUMBERS?

Okay, big question: Is it true I should always spell out single-digit numbers? (one to nine) Answer: In general, yes.

Numbers in Technical Reports

But the issue is different in technical writing, which usually follows a new rule that trumps that old rule:

- Use digits to write numbers when accuracy or emphasis is desired, which is most of the time in technical writing.

So when is accuracy or emphasis *not* desired? Here are some examples:

✓ She has a hundred things to do today.	Using digits is like adding:
✗ She has 100 things to do today.	, for which she has a checklist.
✓ He joined the firm five years ago.	Using digits is like adding:
✗ He joined the firm 5 years ago.	today, and here's his certificate.

There are numbers for which we almost always assume accuracy is desired:

date:	May 6	money:	$2
time:	4 p.m.	percentage:	2 percent
ratio:	3-to-1 odds	page number:	page 4
score:	7 to 5	measurement:	6 pounds

More Numbers in Technical Writing

In addition to the new rule, there are time-proven guidelines:

- Only spell out numbers that can be expressed in one or two words.

spell it out	stick with digits
after seventy-three days	after 170 days
for six hundred dollars	for $695
weighed two tons	weighed 3,850 pounds

- Use a combination of digits and words when it will keep things clear.

   ✓ We counted forty 2-pound rats.
   ✓ We counted 40 two-pound rats.
   ✗ We counted 40 2-pound rats.

   Using all digits invites the reader to envision rodents of unusual size.

- Strive for consistency when showing similar counts.

   ✓ They brought two apples, eight oranges, and nine bananas.
   ✗ They brought two apples, 8 oranges, and 9 bananas.
   ✓ The vote was 12 in favor and 3 opposed.
   ✗ The vote was 12 in favor and three opposed.

- Write out numbers that begin sentences. (or rewrite the sentence)

   ✓ Twenty percent of the measurements were in error.
   ✗ 20% of the measurements were in error.
   ✓ We found that 20% of the measurements were in error.

Fractions

- When you need to use a lot of different fractions, strive for a consistent appearance.
  - ✓ The plaque was 10 1/4 inches high, 8 1/8 inches wide, and 1 1/2 inches thick.
  - ✗ The plaque was 10 ¼ inches high, 8 1/8 inches wide, and 1 ½ inches thick.
- When a fraction is an approximation, you should probably write it out.
  - ✓ We siphoned off about half a liter of the sludge.
  - ✗ We siphoned off about 1/2 liter of the sludge.

Decimals

- Avoid overstating precision in decimals.
  - ✗ To generate 20.7 watts at 14.5 volts we will need 1.4276 amps. [→ 1.4]
  - ✗ The barista poured 0.5 cup of Kona for us to sample. [→ half a]
  - ✗ We measured 5.375 inches using a standard ruler. [→ 5 3/8]
  - ✗ I handed him $5.00, but he wanted singles. [→ five dollars]
- Always put a zero in front of a decimal less than one.
  - ✓ We measured 0.72 and adjusted the setting.
  - ✗ We measured .72 and adjusted the setting.

Units of Measure

- Use the singular form when a fraction or a decimal is less than one. (When there is one or less of anything, it's singular, not plural.)

✓ 0.8 ton	✓ 3/4 inch	✓ 0.75 acre
✗ 0.8 tons	✗ 3/4 inches	✗ 0.75 acres

- When a number and a unit of measure combine to form an adjective, use a hyphen.

  ✓ 12-volt charge ✓ 3-day wait ✓ 2-day-old sample

- When a measurement consists of several elements, do not use commas to separate the elements. (The measurement is considered a single unit.)

  ✓ The package weighed 7 pounds 9 ounces.
  ✗ The package weighed 7 pounds, 9 ounces.

- When a unit of measure is abbreviated, the number is always given in digits.

✓ 6 ft	✓ 5 p.m.	✓ 3 lb
✗ six ft	✗ five p.m.	✗ three lb

- If a symbol is used as a unit of measure and is used in a range, include the symbol after each number. If a symbol is not used, write the unit of measure after the range.

✓ 80%-90%	✓ 25°C-35°C	✓ 8" x 10"
✗ 80-90%	✗ 25-35°C	✗ 8x10"
✓ 80 to 90 percent	✓ 25 to 35 degrees Celsius	✓ 8 by 10 inches

Exercise

Find and fix the errors in this section of a technical report.

2. Non-Indigenous Species (NIS) and the Great Lakes

182 NIS have now found a home in the Great Lakes. In 3 studies so far, ballast water was found to be the largest source of NIS, as shown in Fig. one. The locks along the St. Lawrence Seaway admit vessels as large as 225 m long, 24 m wide, and eight meters deep. On average, each vessel has 2800.42 metric tons of ballast water. Exchange at sea replaces 95-99% of the ballast water with seawater. Despite regulations, fifteen new NIS have entered the Great Lakes from ballast water since 1993.

While any NIS may alter the ecosystem, thirteen of the reported NIS have become invasive. The worst of the NIS, the zebra mussel, competes with fish for their food, clogs water intake pipes, and increases toxic algae. Zebra mussels are small, with adults ranging from .3 inches to 1.50 inches long. They live about 4.1 years. Crayfish could have a significant impact on the population of zebra mussels. We watched one crayfish consume one hundred twenty 1 ounce zebra mussels in a single day.

Solution

2. Non-Indigenous Species (NIS) and the Great Lakes

The Great Lakes are now home to 182 NIS. In **three studies so far**, ballast water was found to be the largest source of NIS, as shown in **Fig. 1**. The locks along the St. Lawrence Seaway admit vessels as large as 225 m long, 24 m wide, and **8 m** deep. On average, each vessel has **2800** metric tons of ballast water. Exchange at sea replaces **95%-99%** of the ballast water with seawater. Despite regulations, **15** new NIS have entered the Great Lakes from ballast water since 1993.

While any NIS may alter the ecosystem, **13** of the reported NIS have become invasive. The worst of the NIS, the zebra mussel, competes with fish for their food, clogs water intake pipes, and increases toxic algae. Zebra mussels are small, with adults ranging from **0.3 to 1.5 inches** long. They live **about four years**. Crayfish could have a significant impact on the population of zebra mussels. We watched one crayfish consume **120 one-ounce** zebra mussels in a single day.

FINAL COMMENTS

The advice about writing numbers is generally accepted by those responsible for approving technical reports. For writing numbers in less-technical formats, *The Gregg Reference Manual* is a good resource, because it's both detailed and authoritative.

The best guide to use in writing reports is a recent report that someone else wrote at your company, a report that is viewed as well written. That will give you a good reference for how much material you should include and how you should arrange it.

Regardless of preferred format, there are some things your report should, and should not, do:

- It should:
    - Be concise.
    - Be well structured.
    - Include relevant facts.
    - Contain interesting information.
- It should not:
    - Be full of complicated sentences.
    - Look like it was pasted together.
    - Repeat information or advice.
    - Lecture at the reader.

FAQs

Q: *When is it appropriate to use an outline versus the pyramid of logically-linked statements?*

A: When you are writing to inform or influence, use an outline. When you are writing to persuade, and the argument is complicated and detailed, try the pyramid. Above all, use what works for *you*.

Q: *When I have to write a report, I feel burdened and I worry that I'm going to forget something important. Do you have any tips for those of us who suffer from report-writing anxiety?*

A: Just because writing a report is viewed as a specialized task, doesn't mean it requires specialized skills. It's just writing in a special format. To get past the 'special' part, simply find a suitable template or example to follow. Then fill it in, with nothing more than the writing skills you learned from scribbling through this workbook. Yes, it can be time-consuming. But you're essentially getting paid by the hour, right?

When you start to fill out the template or example, begin by writing down the questions the reader wants answered. It may seem simple or silly, but it can help. Just give it a try. Then, underline the key words in the questions. Refer to these key words as you plan, draft, edit. This helps to make sure that nothing important is left out. And don't be afraid to scratch out a keyword or even a question and replace it with something else as you proceed with the writing. It was only a starting point; you're in charge.

CHAPTER 14

Looking Good

> ***In This Chapter***
>
> - Choose fonts for the whole picture.
> - Try to avoid using justification.
> - Blank space is a design feature: use it.
> - Loosen, list, and layer for readability.

WHY YOU SHOULD CARE

The writer who types large blocks of text with little concern for fonts or formatting leaves the reader with a sea of words that can numb the mind. The writer who is overly concerned with adding visual interest to a document by using a wide variety of fonts bombards the reader with distractions.

Your boss will appreciate it if you can find a balance between boring your readers and shocking them: both situations result in them not really hearing your message. When you make your text truly readable, people will not even notice how readable it is: they will be too busy being impressed by what you had to say.

MORE THAN FONT

When we type words into a document, we typically don't give much thought to what the software is doing. It's choosing things for us: font, line spacing, paragraph spacing, column width, and more. Is the program always doing the best thing for us? Absolutely not. It tries, but if it had its way we would all be using the same formats for everything.

This is all well intentioned. It's just software companies trying to give us a decent head start in formatting text for acceptable readability. It's up to us to take it or leave it. And, in general, you should not take it. You should leave it, and tweak things in your text to make it readable.

But what to tweak? Unfortunately, there is no single item you can choose to guarantee good readability. "Always use this font," you might hear from some people. Avoid those people.

To make text readable, you should play with the settings. Only then will you see for yourself what works:

1. Start out small: change a font.
2. Then try changing all the formatting options for a paragraph.
3. When you start using Styles, you will have graduated to the ranks of true professional in making things readable.

Speaking of professionals, please note: Graphic designers and typographers grind their teeth when we call a typeface a font. The words do technically mean very different things. But until you are a graphic designer or typographer, you have no good reason to worry about the distinction. We'll just call it font. Ignore the purists. You have work to do.

A BIT ABOUT FONTS

Font size is the distance from the top of the capital letters to the bottom of the lowercase letters like *y* and *j*.

Font size is given in points. A point is 1/72 of an inch. When you choose a 12 point font, you are choosing to place text inside a horizontal bar that is 12/72 inches high. That is 1/6 of an inch, a bit more than 1/8 of an inch.

General guidelines:

- Fonts between 10 points and 12 points are common in the main text of business documents.
- Smaller fonts, 8 or 9 points, are sometimes used in footnotes or legends for graphics.
- Larger fonts, 14 to 20 points, are most often used for headings and titles.

For large paragraphs of text, the vertical size of letters is not the only thing that matters. What can matter even *more* is x-height: the relative height of the small letter x in relation to the height of capital letters:

> Example of small x-height font: Bodini
> Example of a large x-height font: Georgia

These fonts are the same size: 12 points. The x-height of Georgia makes it seem bigger than Bodini. Therefore, x-height can be a better guide to readability than point size is. However, when you do choose a font with a higher x-height, you usually also have to increase the vertical spacing between lines.

Small x-height fonts are often found in wedding invitations because they are considered elegant. At work, don't worry about elegance; just make it readable.

(Yeah, like, *okay*, there's a lot of fonts! - can't you just <u>tell</u> me which ones are the **best** to use?) Chill, dude. Here's a respectable list of respectable fonts:

serif fonts [serifs are those little flat boots and hats on letters]

Palatino
  Choose the *best* font: Examine x-height by **eye**.
Times New Roman
  Choose the *best* font: Examine x-height by **eye**.
Century Schoolbook
  Choose the *best* font: Examine x-height by **eye**.
Garamond
  Choose the *best* font: Examine x-height by **eye**.
Book Antiqua
  Choose the *best* font: Examine x-height by **eye**.

sans serif fonts

Arial
  Choose the *best* font: Examine x-height by **eye**.
Verdana
  Choose the *best* font: Examine x-height by **eye**.
Franklin Gothic
  Choose the *best* font: Examine x-height by **eye**.
Century Gothic
  Choose the *best* font: Examine x-height by **eye**.
Microsoft Sans Serif
  Choose the *best* font: Examine x-height by **eye**.

Note: these are their industry names; trade names may differ for commercial or copyright reasons.

Monospaced fonts, where every character sits in an invisible box of the same width, were originally created for mechanical typewriters. They are appropriate in a few situations. One is when a judge is telling you he wants all court filings in 12 point Courier. Another is when you need good vertical tracking while writing computer code. Lucida Console or Monaco are fonts often used there. Otherwise, monospaced font is harder to read than other fonts. Avoid it if you can, kind of like the flu.

THE BEST FONT?

What is the most readable font? You might as well ask: What is the prettiest flower? There is no answer to this question. But there are time-proven guidelines:

- For large blocks of text, use a serif font with respectable x-height and ample line spacing.
- For headings, use a larger sans serif type, and put more space above it than below it to make it belong to what follows.

Generally speaking, when you want your reader to sit back, relax, and get into the reading, use a serif font with respectable x-height, and when you want your reader to sit up, take notice, and do what you say, use a sans serif font.

EMPHASIS

Here we're talking about *italic*, **bold**, <u>underline</u>, and color.

Use emphasis sparingly. When you emphasize too much, you emphasize nothing. Non-flashy text is best: readers don't enjoy being shouted at.

Guidelines for not going overboard with font emphasis:

- Large sections of text in italics are known to reduce reading speed. The stories in this book use italics to entice you to relax and enjoy the show.
- Underlines are garish and bring to mind your great grandparents' manual typewriters.
- Using a variety of colors for text is appropriate if you are advertising for the circus. In you're writing at work, try to only use it to help readers navigate through the document. Maybe use it to highlight headings.

STYLES

Learn a few things about using the Styles feature in your word processing software. You will be surprised at how much time it can save. With a single click you can transform the text of a whole paragraph.

LINE SPACING

Line spacing is also measured in points. Typically, line spacing is 2 or 3 points taller than font size. If line spacing is too small, readers have to work too hard, and they can get lost when locating the start of the next line. Also, fonts with large x-height tend to need larger line spacing, and vice versa.

COLUMN WIDTH

If there are more than 12 words per line, readers tend to lose their place, read more slowly, or have poorer retention. The reported reason for this is that the reader actually has to engage more eye and neck muscles to read wider lines. Or, if more words are crammed into an acceptable line length using a smaller font, it's hard to read the words.

Lines that are too short cause the reader to read with an unusual rhythm. Oddly, shorter lines cause readers to skip ahead to the next line more readily, often before finishing the short line.

GIVE IT SPACE

White space:

- Use generous margins and reasonable space between columns.
- Many people feel the need to fill white space with type. Resist this urge. It's okay to leave blank space on a page.

Paragraph spacing:

- This is most useful when first lines are not indented. But avoid using so much space that the paragraphs look like independent islands.

Heading spacing:

- Place more open space above a heading than below it. Make sure it looks like it belongs with the text it introduces.

JUSTIFICATION, OR NOT

Justification means making things vertically even on the left side and on the right, by inserting spaces between words so that the lines of text take up the full column width. Reasons given for this include economy and neatness. These are weak excuses and have little to do with readability. Of course if your boss insists on it, you have no choice. But there are true reasons to not justify the text in your writing at work, and they all have to do with readability.

Justified text can create vertical, unsightly puddles and wandering rivers inside your paragraphs:

Nearly 25 percent of households have on-site wastewater treatment systems, and 15 percent get their drinking water from private wells. Communities have not established adequate programs to ensure proper functioning of onsite systems for wastewater treatment and private drinking water wells.

This is not good. Without justification, word spacing remains constant:

Nearly 25 percent of households have on-site wastewater treatment systems, and 15 percent get their drinking water from private wells. Communities have not established adequate programs to ensure proper functioning of onsite systems for wastewater treatment and private drinking water wells.

This is good. Your readers are more relaxed. Also:
- They read word to word with less effort.
- They read line to line with less effort.
- They read faster.
- They read with better comprehension.

In short, it's all good.

Exercise

Critique each paragraph for the readability of its text:

It was the best of times, it was the worst of times, it was the age of wisdom, it was the age of foolishness, it was the epoch of belief, it was the epoch of incredulity, it was the season of Light, it was the season of Darkness, it was the spring of hope, it was the winter of despair, we had everything before us, we had nothing before us, we were all going direct to Heaven, we were all going direct the other way - in short, the period was so far like the present period, that some of its noisiest authorities insisted on its being received, for good or for evil, in the superlative degree of comparison only.

There were a **king** with a <u>large</u> jaw and a **queen** with a <u>plain</u> face, on the throne of England; there were a **king** with a <u>large</u> jaw and a **queen** with a <u>fair</u> face, on the throne of France. In both countries it was clearer than crystal to the **lords** of the State preserves of loaves and fishes, that things in general were settled for <u>ever</u>.

Solution

Note: No corrections were made to the paragraphs. We're just having fun being critical and pointing out how someone might do a bad job of typesetting for the first two paragraphs of the novel *A Tale of Two Cities* by Charles Dickens.

It was the best of times, it was the worst of times, it was the age of wisdom, it was the age of foolishness, it was the epoch of belief, it was the epoch of incredulity, it was the season of Light, it was the season of Darkness, it was the spring of hope, it was the winter of despair, we had everything before us, we had nothing before us, we were all going direct to Heaven, we were all going direct the other way - in short, the period was so far like the present period, that some of its noisiest authorities insisted on its being received, for good or for evil, in the superlative degree of comparison only.

- Large x-height font should have large line spacing.
- Large blocks of *italic* font slows reading speed.

There were a **king** with a <u>large</u> jaw and a **queen** with a <u>plain</u> face, on the throne of England; there were a **king** with a <u>large</u> jaw and a **queen** with a <u>fair</u> face, on the throne of France. In both countries it was clearer than crystal to the **lords** of the State preserves of loaves and fishes, that things in general were settled for <u>ever</u>.

- Small x-height font should have small line spacing.
- Justification is almost always a bad idea.
- Emphasis (**bold**, <u>underline</u>) can be distracting.

Chapter 14 ~ Looking Good

LAYOUT: WHAT'S GOOD?

It's subjective. The best way to decide what makes for good layout is to study documents at work. Which ones are easy to read? Which ones aren't? In the difference, you will discover what makes for good layout. And then you can adjust the layout of your documents using well-chosen guidelines.

Three easy steps can change dense blocks of text into clearly-presented content:

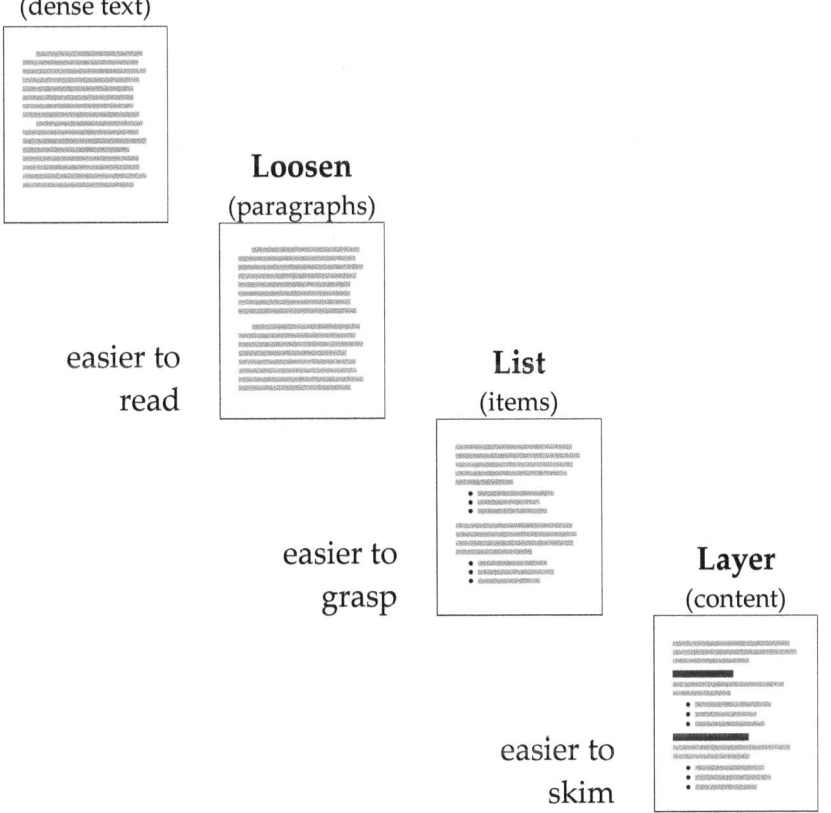

Loosen: People expect dense text in a novel, something they read when they have plenty of time. At work, few people have the luxury of time. Information should be presented in logical chunks, in physically-separated blocks. When you can, break up long paragraphs into shorter ones, and put extra space between them.

List: Busy readers at work are much more likely to read through a group of similar items if they are reformatted from paragraph form into a list.

Layer: A document with layered content allows busy people to read only parts of it but still get the gist of it.

All together:

> Total Summary - The first sentence should give them a summary of the entire document.
>
> **Heading** - The next thing they might skim through are section headings, which should each be an engaging summary of a chunk of the content. Bold font can help.
>
> Chunk Summary - Under each heading might be another summarizing sentence.
>
> - Indented List - The detailed information that busy but interested readers could go back to and carefully read another time.

Vertical spaces, bold font, and horizontal indents can all be used to quickly convey "where we are" in the hierarchy of the layered content. Busy readers will thank you!

Exercise

Imagine that you work as a benefits administrator in a Human Resources department. You must alert all employees to changes in benefits, and you must explain to them how to change their benefits if they want to do so.

Chapter 14 ~ Looking Good 241

You wrote a rough draft:

The yearly Open Enrollment for benefits is coming up soon. Please note that new options are available in your benefits. For example, you can opt out of the medical plan if you are already covered by a spouse's plan. Also, you can choose from a wider variety of life insurance payouts. Even the dental plan is changing: employees can now get dental surgery coverage for their family.

Now is your chance to change your benefits. We recommend that you first find out about new options available to you by reading our website. After that you can get a copy of form HR505, fill it out in its entirety, sign it, date it, and send it to me. You must submit the form during Open Enrollment, the first five working days of October.

Now loosen, list, and layer to improve readability:

Solution

> New options are available in your benefits, which you can change during Open Enrollment.
>
> **What are the new benefits?**
>
> Important new benefits include the following:
> You can select from a wider variety of life insurance payouts.
>
> - You can extend dental surgery coverage to your spouse and children.
> - You can opt out of the medical plan if you are already covered by your spouse's medical plan.
>
> **How do I change my benefits?**
>
> We recommend you do the following:
>
> 1. Learn more about your options by reading the internal HR website.
> 2. Fill out all sections of form HR505, then sign and date it.
> 3. Submit the form during Open Enrollment, which is during the first five working days of October.

FINAL COMMENTS

Choices about font and layout are subjective. They can also be cultural. What might be appropriate in a design firm may not be appropriate in a government agency. This book isn't the final authority. Your coworkers are, especially if some of them maintain a writing style manual for the organization.

Psychologists conclude that reading is a dynamic process in which readers actively organize the material in a way that makes sense to them. And if you present them with distracting fonts and inconsistent layout, they will simply give up trying to understand what it is you have to say. Some writers assume that if certain readers didn't get it, those readers were lazy. Try not to fall into that trap; it's the trap of the lazy writer.

FAQs

Q: *I like to use lots of different fonts. It shows I'm creative. What's wrong with that?*

A: If it contributes to what you get paid to do, go for it. If you job description specifically states that you were hired to help the company by creating pretty text, you're in your element.

But if your job doesn't ask for this, you must step back and find a way to admit that pleasing yourself is not what you get paid to do. Try to make a joke about it. Say this: "My job is to make my boss look good." Maybe in the back of your mind you'll hear your quiet self saying, "Okay, okay, it's not about me, I get it." Try to control your need for artistic expression, until perhaps you are asked to prepare a flyer for a company picnic. Then go wild.

Q: *I have no artistic ability at all. I can't tell if the format of my documents is good or not. Any suggestions?*

A: There are several kinds of format: appearance format and content format. For appearance format, look around (or ask your boss) for documents that are considered good. For content format, follow the advice given in this chapter and others. For emails, play it safe; don't overdo it with fonts and colors. Keep it simple and neat.

SECTION V

Finesse

When your writing at work is correct, clear, concise, and effective, you're way ahead of the game. But if you want to hit it out of the ballpark, you need to excel at courtesy and influence. Coddle the reader? Cajole the reader? It sounds manipulative, right? Maybe so, but these writing techniques are not anything new. You already use them instinctively. Now you will analyze them, label them, and try them. When you become adept at using them, you will be writing with true finesse.

Chapter 15: Tactful Writing – How would you react to a formal letter from a cousin in third grade? How about a chummy email from a CEO you don't know? Tact is knowing your place, but not in a bad way. In a good way. It's handy to know how to adjust your writing so that you don't befuddle or insult your reader.

Chapter 16: Diplomatic Writing – How should you write back to people who are being nasty with you? At home, it's up to you. But at work, it helps to know how to consistently take the high road. Your boss would like that. Here you'll learn techniques for being the professional your boss wants you to be.

Chapter 17: Persuasive Writing – Do you want your hard work to have an impact? Techniques in persuasive writing will be invaluable to you. Some of these techniques are abstract at first, but with practice you'll become the person in the office people come to for advice about making their words more convincing.

Chapter 18: Promotional Writing – Are you in Sales? It doesn't matter. The techniques of promotional writing are applicable to many situations at work. We're not talking about manic wording on junk mail; we're talking about structure and phrasing that promote your company or your work.

~ Subject in Action ~

Angie's first job was at a non-profit organization with a mission she was passionate about. Her first assignment was to write a promotional letter, intended to solicit ads and sponsorships for a fundraising event. She gathered many facts about her organization's programs and accomplishments. She wrote a long appeal letter that was well organized. She proofread the letter several times to make sure it was error free. Angie then took the letter to her supervisor, anticipating praise for her efforts. But after reading the letter, her supervisor looked up and said, "This is thorough, accurate, well organized ... and, unfortunately, boring. I'm sorry, but because we have to get this out immediately, I'll have to write it myself." Angie was crushed. And she was frustrated with the lack of direction. All she could do was try to learn from how her supervisor wrote the letter.

CHAPTER 15

Tactful Writing

> **In This Chapter**
>
> - Style is how *you* write.
> - Tone is what *they* hear.
> - Be as direct as your *position* allows.
> - Be as personal as your *purpose* allows.

WHY YOU SHOULD CARE

It's bad when you offend a reader—really bad if the situation is important to your boss. You must be tactful. You must control your writing style. You must strive to assemble your words so the reader will naturally conclude that your tone is acceptable. You're writing for a colleague, not a professor. Teachers graded you on correctness; people at work will also judge you on appropriateness. And their disapprovals don't disappear at the end of a semester. Worse yet, they can show up in a performance review, a record that never goes away.

STYLE VERSUS TONE

When speaking face-to-face, you communicate in two ways:

1. Language (what you say)   2. Tone (how you say it)

When you communicate using only typed words, you are at a disadvantage regarding tone. You must adjust the style of your language to the reality of the written word:

Style is how *you* write.   <u>But:</u>   Tone is what *they* hear.

Your reader opens your document and immediately wonders:

- **Who is this from?**
    - Is this person a superior of mine? About the same level as me? Subordinate?
    - What is their relative **position** of power?
- **What is this about?**
    - Is this a request or a recommendation? A negative response, or just informational?
    - What is the **purpose** of this writing?

Your reader then makes subtle judgments about your tone:

Are the words and sentences appropriate for the **position** of this writer? Are the words and sentences appropriate for the **purpose** of this writing?	Yes →	I approve of this writer's tone.

But how do you adjust your style to get the right tone? The not-so-helpful answer is that you already do it intuitively, though seldom perfectly. An analytical answer can be found in the Position and Purpose Guidelines on the next two pages.

POSITION GUIDELINES

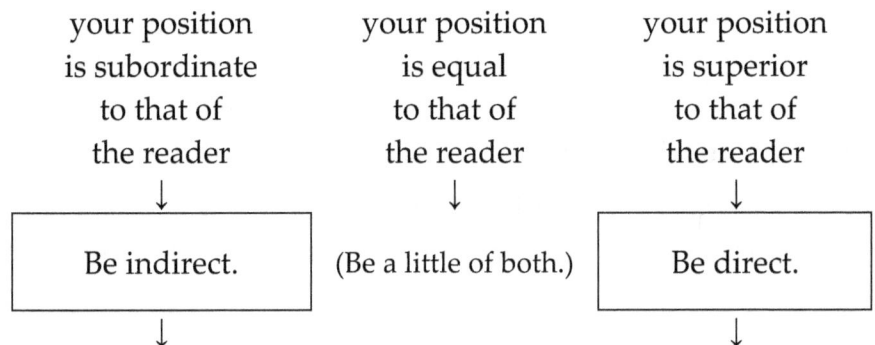

Use complex sentences.

Before investing any more time and money analyzing all the options, it should be verified that the customer remains committed to the project.

Avoid imperatives.

It would be best if questions were received before Friday.

Hide accountability.

After discussions about schedules, the meeting was postponed.

Use hedging words.

almost, a little, maybe, perhaps, possibly, it seems, some might conclude

Use simple sentences.

We need to know if our customer is still committed to the project.

Use imperatives.

Send me your questions by Friday.

Show accountability.

Bob decided to postpone the meeting.

Avoid hedging words.

To control your writing this way, you have to consciously step away from your personal writing style preferences. It's no longer about you: it's for the reader and the situation. You may also notice that here, appropriateness trumps clarity.

PURPOSE GUIDELINES

It's seldom that your purpose in writing can be accurately described by a single word. Nevertheless, four reasonable examples are provided below. Your intuition will guide you in placing yourself on the continua of negative/positive and guarded/friendly that help define how personal you should be.

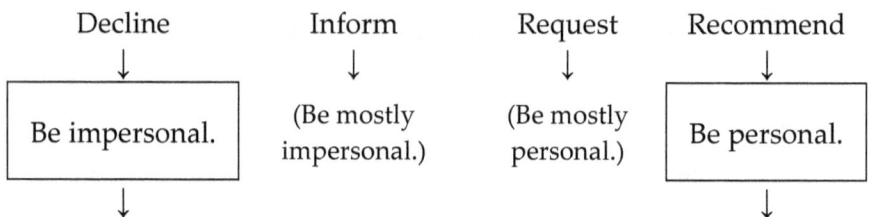

Decline ↓	Inform ↓	Request ↓	Recommend ↓
Be impersonal.	(Be mostly impersonal.)	(Be mostly personal.)	Be personal.

Use formal sentences.

This is to inform you that the proposal was delivered to the Director of Accounting.

Use titles, not names.

WidgeKo's president attended the meeting.

Avoid personal pronouns.

The presentation was informative.

Avoid contractions.

We are disappointed that WidgeKo's president will not attend the next meeting.

Use conversational sentences.

I handed your proposal to my boss.

Use names, not titles.

Parker Mansfield attended the meeting.

Use personal pronouns.

I learned a lot at your presentation.

Use contractions.

We're disappointed that Parker won't attend the next meeting.

Chapter 15 ~ Tactful Writing

Exercise

Imagine you're a salesperson at Radnor Inc., a medium-sized printer, and you're writing to Dana Swansea, a marketing manager at Glamorgan Inc., a large retailer. You're writing to turn down the opportunity to print the Glamorgan catalog.

Complication: Jordan Penarth, who works for Dana Swansea at Glamorgan, is a family friend, and you told Jordan you would welcome a chance to print the catalog. Your goal is to leave the door open for other printing jobs in the future.

Assume: position = subordinate, so be indirect
purpose = decline, so be impersonal

Now, write a brief letter, making up any details:

Ms. Swansea:

Solution

position = subordinate, so be indirect

purpose = decline, so be impersonal

Ms. Swansea:

Last week a request was received to print the Glamorgan catalog. It seems, however, that the timing was off a little because, given the need for a long lead time, the schedule for printing the catalog cannot be met.

Perhaps it might be helpful to enter discussions about other opportunities to work together on printing jobs that periodically arise. For example, because Radnor excels at delivering high-quality sales brochures for large retailers, it would be beneficial to stay in touch.

Respectfully,

Be indirect:	
(1) Use complex sentences.	3 of 4 sentences use 20+ words
(2) Avoid imperatives.	none
(3) Hide accountability.	did not mention Jordan
(4) Use hedging words.	4: seems, a little, perhaps, might
Be impersonal:	
(1) Use formal sentences.	lots of passive voice
(2) Use titles, not names.	no names of people
(3) Avoid personal pronouns.	none used
(4) Avoid contractions.	none used

Chapter 15 ~ Tactful Writing   253

Exercise

Imagine you're the CIO at Cardigan, Inc., a large manufacturer, and you're writing a letter to Devin Newport who works for Cardigan at a small division at another location. You're writing to ask that they try the new accounting program.

Complication: Jessie Chepstow, who works for Devin Newport, used to work at headquarters, but was asked to leave. Jessie has been spreading false rumors that the new program is full of bugs. Your goal is to get all company divisions to confidently adopt the new program.

Assume: position = superior, so be direct
          purpose = recommend, so be personal

Now, write a brief letter, making up any details:

Dear Devin,

Solution

position = superior, so be direct

purpose = recommend, so be personal

> Dear Devin,
>
> First of all, congratulations on your promotion. I hear your division is growing and will need to upgrade its IT capabilities. Try our new accounting program. I promise you're going to love it. It's better, faster, and easier to use.
>
> I hope you know that any claims about bugs by Jessie Chepstow were due to personal issues, and have no basis in fact. It's no big deal, though. We're confident our testing has perfected the program. Call for more information.
>
> Regards,

Be direct.	
(1) Use simple sentences.	7 of 9 sentences under 10 words
(2) Use imperatives.	2
(3) Show accountability.	mentioned Jessie
(4) Avoid hedging words.	none used
Be personal.	
(1) Use conversational sentences.	all
(2) Use names, not titles.	1
(3) Use personal pronouns.	avg about 1 per sentence
(4) Use contractions.	4

OTHER KINDS OF TACT

What about sticky situations? What tactful words can help when things could become embarrassing?

First of all, consider not writing anything at all. What if your boss wrote something that you know is wrong. Don't respond in writing. Talk in person, discreetly: "That's interesting what you wrote. I was thinking the same thing. But I recently learned about another way of looking at it."

When a coworker needs an answer in writing, being tactful is definitely an acquired art. Consider three situations:

1. A coworker presents an idea that's seriously flawed.

Don't discourage him, but do redirect him: "That's an interesting way to look at it. But I wonder if X would make it difficult." "Interesting – that sounds like something that would be even better for our Y department, because of Z."

2. A coworker expects you to do something unpleasant.

Acknowledge the expectation, and explain why you can't meet it. "I appreciate your assigning me X, but I have to say I'm not comfortable with Y. I could help gather Z, but I can't participate any further than that. Sorry."

3. A coworker requests a critique of his awful writing.

Compliment the effort. If you do want to help him, suggest how you would improve it if it had been your own writing. "I liked your analysis of X. Every time I get that far, I always find inspiration in *Hit the Job Writing* to make it shine." "It was very thorough. When I prepare reports like that, I often find myself referring to *The Gregg Reference Manual* for guidance."

FINAL COMMENTS

Let's be honest, this is very subjective stuff. And it's icky, touchy-feely stuff. But consider this claim: style counts as much as content, in the mind and feelings of the reader. Judging the situation (position/purpose) accurately might be what separates you from coworkers who don't even try.

FAQs

Q: *These guidelines can suggest conflicting styles. What do I do when I need to be both direct, with simple sentences, and impersonal, with formal sentences?*

A: You compromise and use your best judgment. When in doubt, avoid extremes in either direction.

Q: *When I write an email, I'm usually confident the style is appropriate. But sometimes I have this nagging feeling that it's not quite right. Should I trust my skills and send it? Or trust my feelings and re-write it?*

A: Trust your feelings. Save the email in a text file. Come back to it tomorrow. Here's a guarantee: two out of five times you do this, you will sigh with relief at how it saved your bacon.

CHAPTER 16

Diplomatic Writing

> **In This Chapter**
>
> - Respond to nastiness with control.
> - Be the Earth: firmly address.
> - Be the Wind: gently redirect.
> - Be the Fire: and disappoint your mom.

WHY YOU SHOULD CARE

Diplomacy is not just about graciousness or compromise. Under the worst circumstances—when someone is attacking you—diplomacy is about how your behavior reflects your employer's ideals and affects your employer's reputation. Don't go into situations planning to 'wing it' if things happen to get ugly. Be prepared, by trying the exercises in diplomatic writing. It'll only take a few minutes.

OH MY ...

You have just received one of *those* emails at work. Let's be kind and call it heated. What do you do? And how do you do it in a way that protects you and your employer?

There are three ways you can reply to heated email:

Earth - firmly address

Wind - gently redirect

Fire - angrily react

The **Earth** approach (firmly address) is appropriate when you have to deal with an in-house bully. It uses three steps:

Mindset: Be the Wall.	• No one has the right to insult me. • I am going to let him know this is not okay. • I'm going to hold him accountable so he doesn't do this again.
Actions: Do the You.	• Use the word *you* to identify behavior that is out of line. • Use the word *you* to suggest a correction to that behavior.
Details: Don't overdo.	• Be brief when explaining your rationale.

Chapter 16 ~ Diplomatic Writing   259

The **Wind** approach (gently redirect) is appropriate when you have to deal with a complaining customer.

Mindset: Be no One.	• I am an impartial conduit between this person and my organization. • My boss and everyone else in my organization are supportively standing by. • My words will be viewed not as mine, but as the words of anyone in my organization.
Actions: Say it as they see it.	• Write with *empathy* about *his* situation. • React to what he *means*, not to what he says.
Details: Map it out.	• Put things into perspective by frankly presenting options.

The **Fire** approach (angrily react) is never appropriate at work. Fire destroys, and flaming emails wound. Make mom proud: avoid playing with fire.

USE YOUR WORDS

Here are words to use with the **Earth** approach:

initial reactions	**Do the You.**
Why doesn't he appreciate that I worked hard on that job instead of just criticizing me?	→ We could probably have better results if you pitched in to get the job done.
I may not be a brilliant analyst, but I did the best I could.	→ If you're trying to make me feel bad, it's not going to work.
I hate it when he does that. Why does he have to be so mean?	→ Cut it out. Keep those kind of remarks to yourself.
I've had enough. I don't like to be insulted about my opinions.	→ You have gone too far. Your insults aren't going to change my mind.
I'm not comfortable being rushed.	→ You'll get the report tomorrow.

Here are words to use with the **Wind** approach:

initial reactions	**Say it as they see it.**
Should we call this guy's mommy to give him a time out?	→ I certainly don't blame you for being upset. I'd be upset, too. But we'll work this out.
What a paranoid thing to claim! I had no idea he was supposed to attend the meeting.	→ Let me be sure I understand what you're saying: You're feeling angry because you believe I purposely omitted you from the meeting.
It's not my fault.	→ Believe me, sir, I understand the frustration of having that happen.
I wish he would calm down and be reasonable.	→ Give me something more to work with, and I'll see what I can do to fix that problem.
It's just a purchase order. Why is he screaming?	→ I am confident that we can resolve the problem with your purchase order.

Exercise

Reply to the following email. Use the Earth approach.

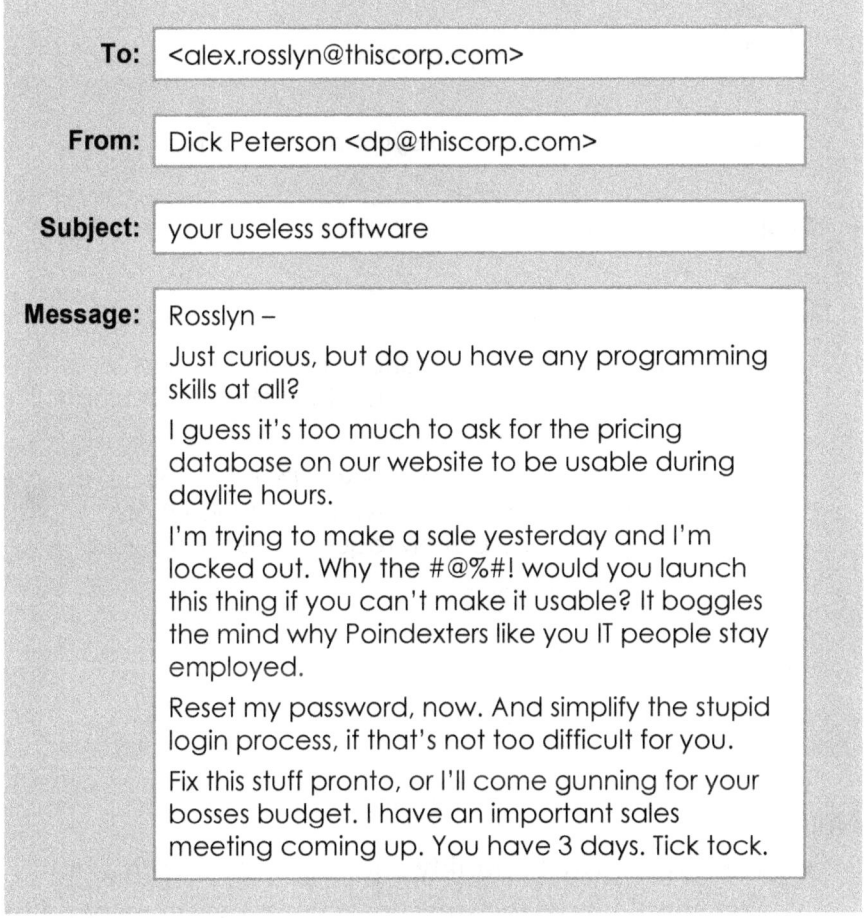

Assume:
- You are responsible for the software and for replying.
- All salespeople received training with the database. They all entered their own passwords as well as backup personal questions and answers.
- Web server logs show that Dick Peterson had tried to log in multiple times and also failed to correctly answer his own personal questions when trying to retrieve his password.

Solution

Some suggestions, using the Earth approach.

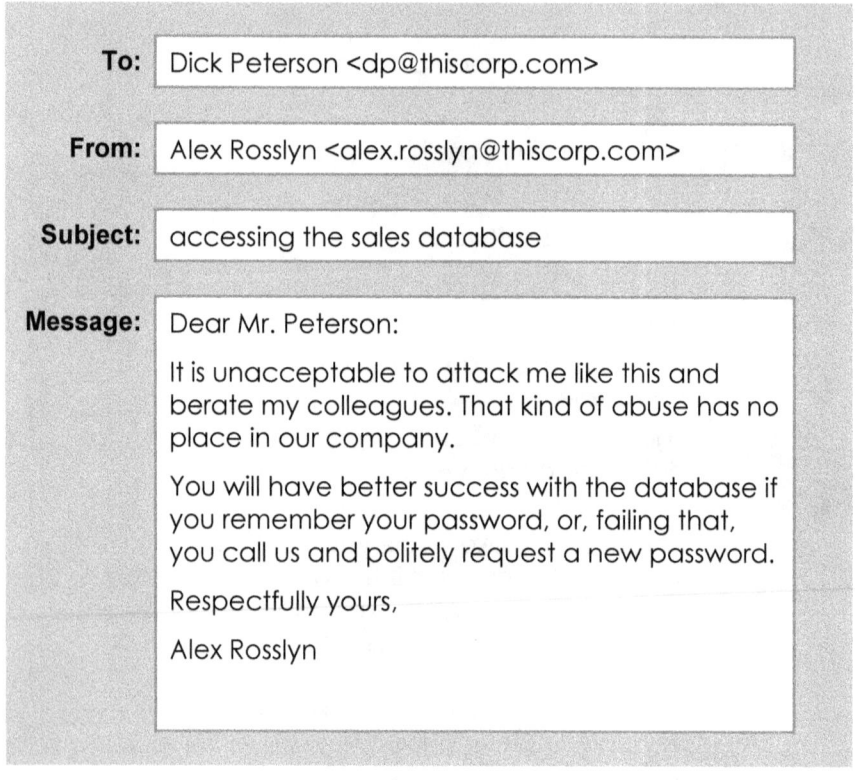

To: Dick Peterson <dp@thiscorp.com>

From: Alex Rosslyn <alex.rosslyn@thiscorp.com>

Subject: accessing the sales database

Message:

Dear Mr. Peterson:

It is unacceptable to attack me like this and berate my colleagues. That kind of abuse has no place in our company.

You will have better success with the database if you remember your password, or, failing that, you call us and politely request a new password.

Respectfully yours,

Alex Rosslyn

Notes:
- This is one way to frankly and firmly deal with a bully. You should have the support of your boss to respond in this fashion.
- This is also a way to openly—for the public record—record when a person was being a bully. Your employer's attorneys should not have a problem with you identifying bad behavior.
- If you or your boss find this approach too confrontational, you have a backup: the Wind approach.

Exercise

Reply to the following email. Use the Wind approach.

To: Jordan Dove <jordan.dove@omnicard.com>

From: Duke Brazen <dukebraz@grrmail.com>

Subject: somebody wake up and fix this

Message:
RE: # 78573937663

Two months ago I paid the balance on my OmniCard. But STILL it doesn't show as paid, and STILL your charging me interest.

HHHEEELLLLLLLLLLOOOOOO !!!

Is anybody THERE? I called the 800 number and got nothing but hand waving from customer service peons.

Do I have to sue you people for 20 million dollars before I get your attention?

Assume:
- You are responsible for investigating and replying to customer complaints.
- This message has been forwarded to you from the company's website. Lucky you.
- You checked and double-checked, and concluded that your company never received the check that this customer claimed to have sent.

Solution

Some suggestions using the Wind approach.

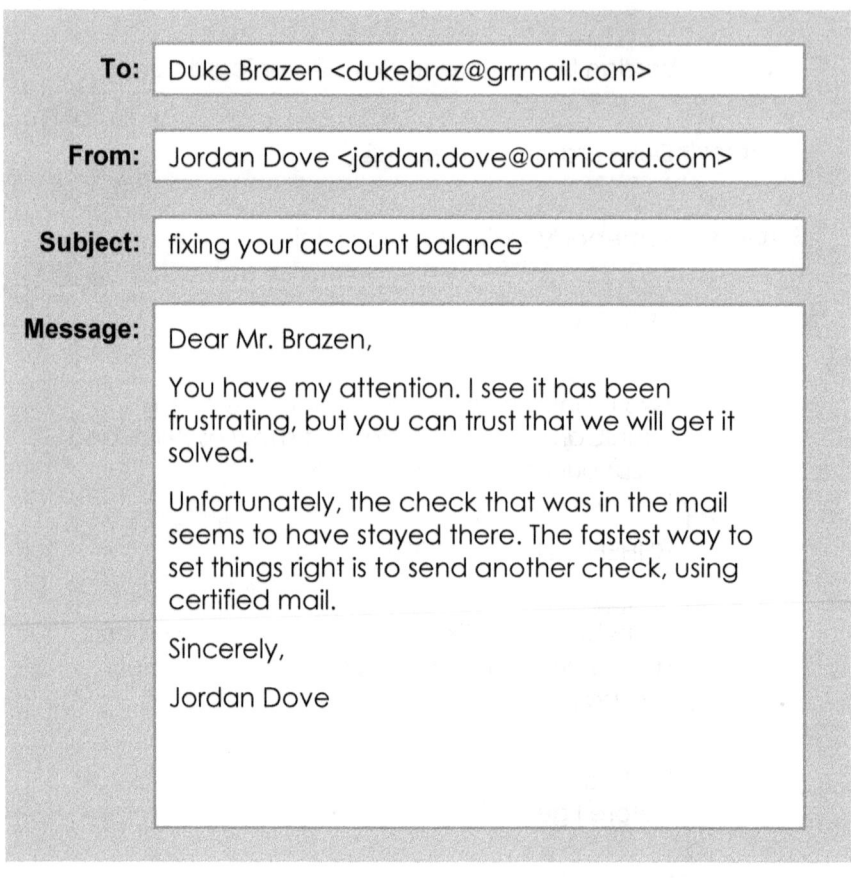

FINAL COMMENTS

You didn't think a chapter on diplomatic writing would be so focused on how to deal with difficult people, did you? Sorry. But the truth is, you may on occasion be judged on how well you deal with those who seem intent on behaving badly. Having tried the Wind and the Earth, you now have techniques in the back of your mind, ready to use if necessary.

Few people have "dealing effectively with jerks on a daily basis" in their job description. If things get really bad, keep in mind that the ultimate responsibility for how your employer responds is the job of its supervisors and its attorneys. Don't be afraid to tell them. They will take your emails seriously.

Dealing with nasty people at work is a topic worthy of a whole book, and there are many out there. Two good ones come to mind: *Verbal Judo* by George Thompson and *Take the Bully by the Horns* by Sam Horn.

FAQs

Q: *Is it ever appropriate to flame out on someone? It seems like that's the only way some people will listen.*

A: At work, absolutely not. But the frustration is understandable. When badly-behaving people just won't listen and keep sending nastygrams in email, don't flame it on—pass it on. Start sending courtesy copies of your responses to your boss and to the person's boss. Your boss will recognize that you are capable of restraint and professionalism. Also, that person's boss should communicate with your boss, not with you, to address the issue.

Q: *I'm afraid people will think I'm weak if I use the Wind approach, even if it's the appropriate way to respond. Can you use the Wind approach and be strong at the same time?*

A: One name: Steven Segal (minus the guns). Strong? Or weak? When someone attacks him, he usually steps aside and calmly assists the attacker in learning that he's only going to hurt himself. Mr. Segal uses his aikido skills to be the Wind. He only resorts to breaking bones when attackers won't quit. Try not to follow that part of his example.

Part of the power of the Wind approach is the ever-present threat that the carefully-controlled breeze could explode into a tornado. If it'll help: you are the tornado, standing back and controlling the gentle Wind at a distance.

CHAPTER 17

Persuasive Writing

> **In This Chapter**
>
> - Speak your reader's language.
> - Adjust strategy to circumstances.
> - Remember primacy and recency.
> - Use rhythm to make an impression.

Why You Should Care

Let's say you write with no errors. And your style is clear and easy to read. In college that was often enough, because you usually had only to *prove* to your professor that you got the right answer.

Now you're at work, and you have to *convince* your boss that your conclusion is the best conclusion, for your boss, for your division, and for the continued economic viability of your employer. Even more, you have to *motivate* your boss to *act*. A lot is on the line. Being persuasive counts.

A THEORY OF PERSUASION

To persuade readers, you must first gain their trust. A subtle but effective way to do this is to speak their language: use words and phrases that match their personality. First identify which side of each personality trait is more evident:

personality: <u>Source</u> of their motivation	
relies on self (The source of their motivation is *internal*.)	**defers to others** (The source of their motivation is *external*.)
language they use:	
I know, it's up to me, I'll gather information and then decide, I'll try it out and see what I think, I know when I have done well	experts say, others recommend, studies show, these references, they should tell us, well respected, their feedback tells me

personality: <u>Direction</u> of their motivation	
achieves goals (The direction of their motivation is *toward objectives*.)	**solves problems** (The direction of their motivation is *away from obstacles*.)
language they use:	
accomplish, achieve, attain, get, obtain, make some progress, let's finish, meet our milestones, what I want, that'll allow us to	fix, solve, prevent, eliminate, avoid, get rid of, it's not perfect, let's find out what's wrong, won't have to deal with

Note: About 20% of people show both sides of these traits. For them, your job is easier: use language from both sides of their motivations, choosing words customized to any situation.

LET'S GIVE IT A TRY

So how do we put this theory into practice? Use a simple sequence of three steps:

1. Listen to their words.
2. Identify their personality.
3. Speak their language.

Example: Imagine it's 1996 and you're a market research analyst, commissioned by DreamWorks to study audience reaction to a movie concept. Your research indicates that they should move forward with the project, an animated film about a sweet young ogre who lives in a swamp. You need to know how to present your results most effectively. You decide to ask Steven Spielberg first.

Here is your email:

We have completed our study of the market potential for the new film. To clearly communicate our results, we need an answer to the basic question: How do you choose which movies to make? Your response will help us write our final report.

Here is the email response from Steven Spielberg:

I read the script and start thinking about why people might enjoy the film. It's always good to fix plot problems early and to anticipate any difficulties with animation technology. But I make my final decision based on the human and emotional possibilities in the story.

Here is our analysis:

language:		personality:
I read the script .. I make my decision	→	relies on self
fix problems .. anticipate any difficulties	→	solves problems

Now you must write an executive summary for the report you will submit to Steven Spielberg. Here is a reasonable outline to use as a starting point:

- Issues: The market potential for the new film.
- Details: The viewing audience loved the concept.
- Findings: Move forward with this project.

Using language that matches the observed personality, here is a brief summary:

This report is about the market opportunity for the film about a sweet young ogre who lives in a swamp. You won't be disappointed with the results of our survey. You will find that the audience thought the ogre story was both novel and appealing. However, you should carefully consider fixing several plot points in the script that some people thought were not quite right. With an improved story, your decision should be easier.

relies on self	→	you will find .. you should carefully consider .. your decision
solves problems	→	won't be disappointed .. fixing .. not quite right

Note: You can also use this technique every day at work as you communicate with your coworkers. You may be surprised at how differently and quickly people respond when you use their language.

Exercise

You are assigned to write the executive summary for the other executives at DreamWorks, Jeffrey Katzenberg and David Geffen. You already sent each of them the same email you sent to Steven Spielberg.

Here is the email response from Jeffrey Katzenberg:

> I'll tell you the rule with me. I know a good movie idea when I see it. My intuition is right on. Always reliable. What I want is a special story, lots of emotions. I gotta love it. Of course we study audience reactions first. After that I go after the best talent to make it happen.

Inspect the language of your reader and identify his personality. Then, using his language, write a brief executive summary using the outline from before:

- Issues: The market potential for the new film.
- Details: The viewing audience loved the concept.
- Findings: Move forward with this project.

Be creative. Make up any details you think appropriate.

	language:		personality:
Jeffrey Katzenberg		→	
		→	

Solution

Jeffrey Katzenberg	language:		personality:
	I know .. my intuition .. I gotta love it	→	relies on self
	what I want .. make it happen	→	achieves goals

This report documents our research. You have achieved your goal. The animated ogre was a hit, plain and simple. First, however, you should consider the few negative audience reactions that were observed. Of course you know what works. But this report should help you arrive at your decision.

relies on self	→	you should consider .. you know .. your decision
achieves goals	→	achieved your goal .. arrive

Exercise

Here is the email response from David Geffen:

We are not burdened by bureaucracy. We are prepared to lose money to build the company, and we enjoy the challenge of investigating all kinds of possibilities. For decisions about animated films, Jeffrey is the expert I trust and defer to. Our decision making isn't perfect; it's not an easy thing to do. I help in a supporting role by staying in the background. I avoid being a key person on the line for decisions like this.

Inspect the language of your reader and identify his personality. Then, using his language, write a brief executive summary using the outline from before:

- Issues: The market potential for the new film.
- Details: The viewing audience loved the concept.
- Findings: Move forward with this project.

Be creative. Make up any details you think appropriate.

	language:		personality:
David Geffen		→	
		→	

Solution

	language:		personality:
David Geffen	expert .. trust and defer to	→	defers to others
	not burdened by .. isn't perfect .. not easy .. avoid	→	solves problems

This report is about the market opportunity for a new project at DreamWorks. The audience loved the animated ogre idea. We recommend a careful assessment of the few problems that caused negative audience reactions. This will help your animation experts in avoiding plot blunders and may help you through the difficult process of picking music and selecting talent.

defers to others	→	audience loved .. we recommend .. animation experts
solves problems	→	problems .. avoiding .. difficult process

THINGS TO SAY AND WHEN TO SAY THEM

Circumstances can dictate which strategies are best to use when you're trying to be persuasive:

Sides For a hostile or ambivalent audience, always present both sides. For a friendly audience, use a one-sided argument.

Facts Giving many facts rarely changes attitudes; it only increases the resolve of those who already agree.

Problems If your views might cause problems for your readers, put extra effort into using empathy and tact.

Relevance Make it matter to the reader, and it will be heard. Explain why before saying *therefore*.

Questions Instead of making an assertion, ask a rhetorical question. It makes the reaction personal, which draws the reader in.

Testimonials A testimonial is as effective as the source is "one of us."

Recommendations Credibility is enhanced if you include recommendations.

Hyperbole Credibility is diminished if you use hyperbole.

Do these seem like common sense? Maybe. But they are all valid and worthy of keeping in mind as you write.

MAKE IT FIRST, MAKE IT LAST

To persuade people, use the concepts of *primacy* and *recency*. In the mind of your reader, the idea presented first has primacy and the idea presented last has recency. The ideas you state first and last have a better chance of being remembered than do the ideas placed in the middle.

The example below shows a few lines from the Declaration of Independence by the leaders of the American colonies.

All men are created equal.
The history of the King is a history of repeated injuries.
He has kept among us, in times of peace, standing armies.
He has cut off our trade with all parts of the world.
He has imposed taxes on us without our consent.
He has plundered our seas and burnt our towns.
We declare that these colonies are free.
We pledge our lives.

From this small sample of the text, which parts do you remember?

> Jefferson's primacy message: We are equal to you.
> His recency message: We are deadly serious.

USE RHYTHM TO MAKE AN IMPRESSION

Did you ever have an English teacher who took points off for repetition? You can relax now, you've graduated.

Repetition of phrases and structures works. It creates a rhythm that pulls your readers along. And readers who allow themselves to be pulled along are more likely to remember what it is you had to say and recommend.

Consider the Dedication given by Abraham Lincoln at Gettysburg in 1863. Here it is with repeated phrases in bold and parallel structures underlined:

Four score and seven years ago our fathers brought forth upon this continent, a new **nation, conceived** in Liberty and **dedicated** to the proposition that all men are created equal.

Now <u>**we are**</u> engaged in a great civil **war**, testing whether that **nation**, or any **nation** so **conceived** and so **dedicated**, can long endure. <u>**We are**</u> met on a great battle-field of that **war**. <u>**We are**</u> met to **dedicate** a portion of that field as a final resting place of those who here gave their **lives** that that **nation** might **live**. It is altogether fitting and proper that we should do this.

But in a larger sense, <u>**we can not** dedicate</u>, <u>**we can not** consecrate</u>, <u>**we can not**</u> hallow this ground. The brave men, **living** and dead, <u>**who** struggled **here**</u>, have **consecrated** it, far above our poor power to add or detract. The world will little note nor long remember what we say here, but it can never forget what they did here.

<u>**It is for us**</u>, the **living**, rather <u>**to be dedicated**</u> here <u>**to the**</u> unfinished work which they <u>**who** fought **here**</u> have thus far so nobly advanced. <u>**It is** rather **for us to be** here **dedicated to the**</u> great task remaining before us, — **that** from these honored **dead we** take increased devotion to the cause for which they gave the last full measure of devotion, — **that we** here highly resolve that **these dead shall** not have died in vain, **that the nation shall**, under God, have a new birth of freedom, and **that the** government <u>of the</u> **people**, <u>by the</u> **people**, and <u>for the</u> **people, shall** not perish from the earth.

Looks kind of busy, huh? But it's memorable, and it continues to influence us even today. His attempt to persuade can be seen in his repetition of one word, followed by a subtle but significant replacement, and then his recency message:

$$\text{nation .. nation .. nation .. nation ..}$$
$$\text{nation .. (government) .. shall not perish}$$

FINAL COMMENTS

There are many persuasive writing techniques. Some of the most powerful are surprisingly subtle. This is both art and science, and mastery can only be obtained with persistent attention, careful study, and unavoidable trial and error.

FAQs

Q: *Isn't this "speak their language" kind of manipulative?*

A: If you're going over to the dark side, sure. If you're writing for good, not so much. Consider what you do when you vacation among people who don't speak English. How do you think they really feel when you at least try to speak their language? The technique in this chapter is subtle and usually undetectable, but when it is used respectfully and ethically, it's definitely appreciated by your readers.

Q: *When in the writing process should I be concerned with making my words persuasive?*

A: As early as possible; before you start assembling an outline. If you wait until you are editing to "add the persuasive stuff" it will be more difficult for you to do and less effective on the reader.

CHAPTER 18

Promotional Writing

> **In This Chapter**
>
> - Above all, do not be dull.
> - An honest self-interview helps.
> - Try the BrBrBp Roadmap.
> - Choose words that compel.

WHY YOU SHOULD CARE

If you have taken a job as a sales rep, you need to be good at grabbing and keeping attention with your words. If you're not a sales rep but you want to make any business associate sit up and take notice when reading your words, it's time for you to sit up and take notice: the simple techniques of promotional writing are going to make your life at work much easier than you thought it could be. Give them a try. And keep in mind: persuasive people get promoted.

WRITE TO ENTICE

A good sales letter entices the reader. How can you keep your letter from being dull? Here are three steps to guide you:

1. **ChAMP Interview**
    - to generate some good ideas and useful phrases
2. **BrBrBp Roadmap**
    - to lay out an enticing framework for your letter
3. **Compelling Edits**
    - to fine-tune your words to motivate the reader

1. ChAMP Interview: You should pull together your thoughts about yourself and your business. Interview yourself. Write down your answers to the following questions, using details:

Ch	Choice:	Imagine a customer asks you about your competitors.
	Q:	Why should she choose you instead of them?
A	Advice:	Imagine you have just retired from your successful business.
	Q:	What advice can you give to the person taking over?
M	Myth:	Imagine most people believe a myth about your line of business.
	Q:	How is the myth not true of your company?
P	Praise:	Imagine friends are boasting about your business.
	Q:	What are they saying?

Use this set of questions as a guide, not a checklist. At this stage, creativity is your key to being a compelling writer.

You could add more questions:

I	<u>I</u>mage:	What image best communicates what you are all about?
O	<u>O</u>utlook:	Where do you see your business five years from now?
N	<u>N</u>arrative:	What story do you most often tell people about your business?

Even if a question seems irrelevant, the answer you dream up might inspire an idea or phrase that gives your sales letter that extra sparkle. It's worth the effort.

Interview guidelines

Write it down. Seriously, even if you only scribble on a piece of scrap paper, the act of writing it down helps you to be more creative and productive. While you're doing it, here are a few pointers:

(1) A little goes a long way.

A sentence or two for each part of the Interview is all you need. Too many words is a symptom of too much time and effort spent on self-assessment. This should be fun, not therapy.

(2) Get to the benefit.

It's natural and too easy to let your thinking dwell on the statement, "I'm great at X." Try to take the next step. Describe your greatness in terms of how it leads to *benefits* valued by the reader: "Because I'm great at X, you will be able to Y." Now your message is less of a commercial and more of an invitation.

(2) BrBrBp (pronounced burr-burr-beep) **Roadmap:** Before you draft your letter, take advantage of time-tested formats for enticing readers. Use the following as an outline:

BrBrBp	what you write	how they react
Billboard	Open with a statement that commands attention.	Interesting! What else is in here?
rapport	Mention something you have in common.	That is so true.
Benefit	Describe how your offering helps the reader.	I could really use that.
request	State the action you want, but show how it is quick and painless.	That's easy enough to do.
Billboard	End with another provocative statement, but one that also acts as an incentive to act.	Oh! Maybe I should do that now.
personality	In each element, be enthusiastic, friendly, confident, sincere, and uniquely you.	I can trust this person.

Your map:

- It's okay to modify the roadmap. Every sales letter is different.
- In a letter, the P.S. is an excellent place to put your exit Billboard. People are naturally curious. A surprising number of them will read the P.S. even in a form letter.

Your words:

- If you don't make it clear how easy and painless it is to grant your request, readers have a ready-made excuse for delay and inaction.
- Ideally, showing your personality makes your letters fun to read. When you write in a style that fits you, the reader seldom dismisses your writing as generic ad copy.

3. Compelling Edits: Small changes in wording and style can produce significant improvements in how readers respond.

	to the dictionary		to the point
Choose short words.	~~request~~	→	ask
	~~furnish~~	→	give
	~~concerning~~	→	about
	~~subsequently~~	→	later

	cerebral		visceral
Choose emotional words.	~~for~~	→	because
	~~reply~~	→	answer
	~~learn~~	→	find out
	~~complete~~	→	finish

	downer			upper	
Choose positive words.	~~buy~~	~~order~~	→	new	proven
	~~sell~~	~~difficult~~		free	results
	~~cost~~	~~decision~~		save	discover
	~~less~~	~~failure~~		sale	guarantee

	promised possibility		current reality
Use present tense.	~~You will save X.~~	→	Our clients save X.
	~~We have helped clients Y.~~	→	We help clients Y.
	~~Z will give you results.~~	→	Z gives you results.

	imagined story		matter of fact
Make hypotheticals real.	~~If you have X.~~	→	When you have X.
	~~Suppose you are Y.~~	→	You are Y.
	~~What if you could Z?~~	→	You can Z.

	periodic stop signs		enticing signposts
Use linking words.	~~Service you can trust. It's proven to X. Find out Y, or request information concerning Z.~~	→	Service you can trust. And it's proven to X. But first, find out Y. Or, ask us about Z.

Example

Pretend you are a real estate agent named Sandy Sailor. You are writing a sales letter to Mr. Morgan, someone in your area who owns a valuable property. Without much thought, you wrote a rough draft:

> Dear Mr. Morgan,
>
> Enclosed please find two flyers, one for Breakwater Realty, and one for my listings.
>
> I am writing because houses in your neighborhood are selling well right now. If you were in the market, you could get a great price. It's a difficult decision, I know. If you want, I can furnish appraisal data concerning your property.
>
> When it is time to sell your house, please consider listing with Breakwater Realty. I look forward to hearing from you soon.
>
> Sincerely yours,
> Sandy Sailor

Then you brainstormed on the interview and the roadmap:

ChAMP Interview:

Choice:	No local realtor does what I do. I will not accept more than 4 listings at any one time. That way, I can focus better on selling each client's house.
Advice:	Always explain in detail to potential customers the difference between a typical listing and a listing with you: how hard you work, how efficiently you work, how successful you are.
Myth:	"Once realtors get a listing, they don't do much work." Not me! I give my clients a weekly report on the most important marketing activity: talking to successful local realtors about my listings.
Praise:	Sandy works 24/7. Her clients are always surprised at the price they get for their homes. She could sell sand on a beach. Popular realtors are always talking about her listings.

BrBrBp Roadmap:

Billboard:	You are in a seller's market.
rapport:	Real estate activity in our town has been hopping. I sold a house near yours for 40% more than the owner paid only 2 years ago.
Benefit:	You'll get top dollar. I'll do all the work, while you are in the driver's seat.
request:	Talk to me about how I would sell your house. I guarantee you will be surprised how easy it would be. No commitment, and you will learn a lot.
Billboard:	The Fed adjusts the prime rate next month. Buyers are eager to get current low rates. This works to your advantage at this time.

Nearly-final draft:

Billboard

Dear Mr. Morgan:

When you are in a seller's market, it's always good to consider your options.

rapport

Real estate activity in our town has been hopping. I recently sold a house near yours for 40% more than the owner paid only 2 years ago. The attached flyers illustrate the story.

If people list with me, I promise them:

You will see action, for I only accept a few listings at a time. I focus on what really matters: promoting your property to successful local agents.

Advice
Choice
~~Myth~~

Benefit

You will get top dollar, for I create such strong interest among local agents that you could get competing bids.

Praise
Advice

request

Please call me any time to discuss your options. Breakwater Realty is always open.

Yours truly,

Sandy Sailor

Billboard

P.S. Buyers are rushing to get good loans before the Fed increases the prime rate. For the next month, this works in your favor.

Compelling Edits:

> **Henry Morgan —**
>
> **It's a fact:** <u>You</u> are in a seller's market.
>
> **And** it's always good to consider your options.
>
> Real estate activity in our town **is** hopping. **For example**, I **just** sold a house near yours for 40% more than the owner paid only 2 years ago. The attached flyers **tell** the story.
>
> **When** people list with me, I **guarantee** them:
>
> <u>You see</u> <u>action</u>. **Because** I only accept a few listings at a time, I can focus on what really matters: promoting your property to successful local agents.
>
> <u>You get</u> <u>top dollar</u>. **Because** I create such strong interest among local agents, you **can** get competing bids.
>
> **So**, please call me any time to **talk about** your options. Breakwater Realty is always open.
>
> **— Sandy Sailor**
>
> P.S. Buyers are rushing to get good loans before the Fed **bumps** the prime rate. For the next month, this definitely works in your favor.

Please Note: The **bold font** is used here to highlight the edits. The actual letter would not highlight these words.

288   Hit the Job Writing

Exercise

At a party last week, you met someone who expressed interest in your office supply company. You are now mailing information about your business. Edit your draft cover letter to entice continued reading. Be creative and make stuff up.

> Blair McAllister:
>
> Thank you for your interest in Binders Office Supplies. Attached I have provided our catalog.
>
> We are more than just a source for low cost office supplies. As I hope you'll soon learn, our sales associates make it a top priority to become familiar with you and your business, so we can provide you with the best service possible. I am confident we will make our products and services an integral part of your daily routine.
>
> I look forward to doing business with you.
> Taylor Stemberg

Choice:	
Advice:	
Myth:	
Praise:	

Billboard:	
rapport:	
Benefit:	
request:	
Billboard:	

Billboard

Rapport

Benefit

Request

Billboard

Solution

ChAMP Interview:

Choice:	Besides lowest prices, you will get accurate tracking and proactive replenishing for free.
Advice:	Train your account reps to learn about challenges facing the client and to think about custom solutions. Help them to be problem solvers, not just order takers.
Myth:	Account reps only show up to deliver a Christmas present or to re-sign the contract.
Praise:	We never run out of supplies. And we've given up comparing prices against those of big-box stores. Binder is the best. It's like they're part of the team.

BrBrBp Roadmap:

Billboard:	Zero-effort office supplies: It's real, now.
rapport:	Business in our region is slow. Cutting expenses is common. It's a good time to team with a supplier who offloads some of the cost of doing business.
Benefit:	You'll get low prices, <u>and</u> a proactive partner.
request:	Invite us in to explain our unique supplier partnership. It'll only take 30 minutes.
Billboard:	The first time you invite us in, we bring a free box of paper for every printer in your office.

Final Letter:

	Blair McAllister,
Billboard	Zero-effort office supplies? Yes, it's <u>real</u>.
rapport	We all know business in our region is slow. And cutting expenses is common. So, it's a good time to team with a supplier who offloads some of the cost of doing business.
Benefit	You not only get low prices, you get a proactive partner. Heard it all before? How about this: Your feedback determines our bonus pay for your account rep.
request	Invite us in to explain our unique supplier partnership. It only takes 30 minutes.
	Regards,
	Taylor Stemberg
Billboard	P.S. The first time you invite us in, we bring a free box of paper for every laser printer in your office.

FINAL COMMENTS

Purposely using words to establish rapport, being honest about and addressing unflattering misconceptions (myths), re-writing hypotheticals as if they were real: all these activities are part of being a good salesperson. But what if you're not a salesperson? At a minimum, the writing skills gained by at least trying out these ideas will brighten and enlighten your emails, little by little. You will learn where they are helpful and where they are not. And you will learn how to use words—subtly or not—to promote your ideas, your employer, and yourself.

FAQs

Q: *Besides sales positions, where else would I use this style of writing?*

A: If you take the ideas and tone them down a bit, they can still be used to engage and persuade. When you ask readers to do something, the Compelling Edits are effective. When you write an email or letter to people you don't know, the BrBrBp Roadmap is an excellent starting point. When you pitch a new idea to your boss, you're not only writing to persuade, you're writing to promote yourself—your ability to come up with good ideas and your ability to implement them.

How do you tone it down? Easy: use one normal font, avoid **Holy Cow!** emphasis, and leave out the parts where you tell everyone how wonderful you are.

Acknowledgements

Thank you to Andrea Dolph and Linda Dowd for letting me do this. When I read their book, *Hit the Job Running: Because Landing the Job is the Easy Part*, I felt compelled to write a sequel. Special thanks goes to Dale Bredon, who as one of my first bosses, gently let me know that my writing wasn't so good. Thanks to my business partner, Fujiyo Ishiguro, who must have gotten sick of my writing style as she translated so many market research reports into Japanese. And finally, thanks to my wife Teri who kisses me on the head as I clatter away on my keyboard, engrossed in my writing.

About the Author

Joe Judge spent a lot of years in college, partly to support his habit – playing trumpet. He earned several master's degrees in engineering from Rensselaer and an MBA from Stanford. He's held a variety of jobs (engineer, project manager, entrepreneur, analyst) in a variety of industries (energy, aerospace, internet, civil service) in a variety of places (New Jersey, Yugoslavia, California, Pennsylvania, and very briefly in Greenland).

Joe is a bit of a nerd about writing. For more than two decades he studied writing in two ways: first, by reading many books on the subject; second, by taking on jobs that required a great deal of writing. This workbook is the culmination of efforts that started when he taught business writing in the Stanford Continuing Studies Program. Through personal experience, he believes that to truly improve your writing you should write— in a workshop, in a workbook, or on the job.

Index

A

Abstractions, 118
Active voice, 152-54
    Exercise, 153-54
Adding information to sentences, 167-170
    Conjunctions, 167
    Free modifiers, 168-69
    Subordinate clause, 168
Announcements (documents), 176-180
    Exercises, 177-8, 179-180
Announcements (verbs), 118
Anxiety when writing, 228
Apostrophes, 40-43, 89, 90
    Exercise, 41-2

B

Bad writing
    Email, 195
    Lack of early planning, 208
    Undefined purpose, 5
Bias, 128-32
Bloat, 100-102, 144-45 *(See also Unnecessary Words)*
    Exercise, 101-102
Brainstorm, 11
BrBrBp (Billboard rapport Benefit request Billboard personality) Roadmap, 280, 282-87, 292
    Exercise, 288-91
Brogan, John, 304
Bureaucratic verbs, 111-12
    Exercise, 111-12

C

Capital letters, 48, 231
ChAMP (Choice Advice Myth Praise) Interview, 280-81, 285
    Exercise, 288-91
Charvet, Shelle, 303
Clarity, 6, 121-22
    Benefits of, 97
Clause, 68, 154
    Introductory, 88
    Subordinate, 168
Clear Technical Writing, 304
Clichés, 131
Closing, 176, 181
Colon, 48, 49
Color, 140, 146
Column width, 234
Comma splice, 44
Commas, 44-47, 48, 49, 50, 53, 54, 88, 89, 90
    Exercise, 45-46
Compelling Edits, 283-87
    Exercise, 288-91
Compound sentences and commas, 44, 88, 89
Conciseness, 6, 139-150
Conflicted verbs
    Exercises, 113-14, 115
Conjunction, 44, 53-54, 88, 89, 167
Contractions and apostrophes, 40
    Exercises, 41
Correct punctuation
    Benefits of, 37, 39, 43
    Story, 38

Correct words, 67-82
    Benefits of, 37, 67, 81
Creativity, 31-32, 280

D
Dash, 48
Deadwood, 100-102 *(See also Unnecessary Words)*
    Exercise, 101-102
Diplomacy, 19, 33, 255, 257
    Benefits of, 247
Diplomat and Director, 19-23, 33
    Exercise, 22-23
Distractions, 118
Drafts, 29-30, 140-148
Drivel, 131-132
    Exercise, 132

E
Earth response to heated email, 258, 260
    Exercise, 261-62
Editing, 122, 140-48, 283-91
Effective Writing
    Story, 96
Email, 176, 194, 195-206, 256, 258, 265, 292
Email Message, 196-200
    Contractions 199
    Opening & Closing, 196-97
    Paragraphs, 200
    Punctuation, 199
    Request Etiquette, 197
    Response Etiquette, 198
    Tricky nice words, 198
    Typing, 199
Email subject line, 200-204, 205
    Exercise, 203-204
Emoticons, 206

Emphasis, 233
English as a second language, 66
Essential English Grammar, 304
Ewing, David, 81, 304

F
Filler, 140-41
Fire response to heated email, 258, 259
Flow, 158-60
Fonts, 230-33, 243, 244
Formality, 122
Formatting
    Benefits of, 229
    Emphasis, 233
    Exercise, 237-38

G
Galbraith, John Kenneth, 99
Grammar, 55-66, 67-82, 83, 84-94, 116, 154, 168, 199, 208
    Alignment to story, 116-17
    Checker, 54
    Proofreading, 87
Gregg Reference Manual, 93,189, 227, 255, 304
Gucker, Philip, 304

H
Homonyms, 71-74, 82, 88
    Exercise, 73-74
Hooks, 157
Horn, Sam, 265, 304
Hyphen, 50

I
IC-WaWa technique, 68
Idea generation, 6

Idioms, 75-80
    Exercises, 75-76, 77-78, 79-80
Ignorance of English, 81
Imprecision, 146
Infinitives, 75
Inspection report, 213
Introductory elements and commas, 44, 88
Introductory modifier, 90
Inviting writing, 161

J
Justification, 235-36

L
Layout, 239-42, 243,244
    Exercise, 241-42
Letters, 176, 181-82, 193, 194, 292
    Exercise, 181-82
Line & Link Game, 57-58
    Exercise, 59-60
Line spacing, 234
Links, 158
Logoria, 140-41

M
Matching Words, 55-66
    Benefits of, 55, 65
    Modifiers, 63-64, 65
    Pronouns, 61-62
    Verbs, 56-60
Memos – *See Announcements*
Message, 2, 9, 10, 38, 96, 100, 123, 133, 135, 136, 172, 194, 195, 196-206, 229, 261, 262, 263, 264, 276, 278, 281
Mind mapping, 11-12
Mistakes, common, 88-90

Modifiers, 63-64
    Exercise, 63-64
Motivation, 268-74
    Exercises, 271-72, 273-74
Mumbo Jumbo, 131, 138

N
Negations, multiple, 124
Negative phrasing, 124, 145
Negative words, 124, 137
Negativity, 124-27
Numbers in Technical Reports, 221-26
    Accuracy, 221
    Decimals, 223
    Exercise, 225-26
    Fractions, 223
    Units of Measure, 224

O
Opening sentences, 16-18, 34-36
Ordering, 20
Organization, 15, 19-28
Outline, 15, 24, 30, 33, 35, 208, 227
    Exercises, 25-28

P
Parallels, 90, 154-56, 176
    Exercise, 155-56
Parentheses, 48
Passive Voice, 152-54, 171
    Exercise, 153-54
Persuading on Paper, 303
Persuasive strategies, 275
Persuasive writing, 172
Phrase, 33, 63, 100, 122, 128, 140, 150, 181, 193, 268
    Bloated, 144

Idiomatic, 75
Introductory, 49
Negative, 145
Politically correct, 128, 138
Prepositional, 50, 162
Redundant, 107, 109
Repetition of, 277

Phrase (*continued*)
Singular, 56
Unnecessary, 100, 103
Verb, 111

Planning to write (*See also up-front thinking*)
Benefits of, 15, 33-34

Plurals and apostrophes, 40, 89
Political correctness, 138
Ponderous writing, 99

Positive words
Benefits of, 123, 137

Possession and apostrophes, 40
Practice, 14, 55, 83, 90, 95, 134, 172, 175, 185, 246, 269
Prepositions, 50, 75, 86, 162-66
Presentations, 183-86
Exercises, 183-84, 185-86
Primacy, 276
Productivity, 97
Professional, 16, 99, 199, 230, 245
Progress report, 214
Exercise, 215-218
Project completion report, 214
Pronouns, 61-62, 65, 88, 89, 90
Bias, 128
Exercise, 61-62
Proofread, 82, 83, 87-94
Techniques, 87
Puffery, 117
Punctuation, 39-54 (*See also Correct Punctuation*)

Email, 199
Exercise, 51-52
Purpose for writing, 4-6, 11-12, 13, 176
Pyramid: concise writing, 140-48
Pyramid logic, 208-210, 227
Exercise, 209-210

R

Reader
And subject, 35
And writing purpose, 5
Depiction, 9-10
Description, 7-9
Ease of reading, 97-99
Focused writing, 133
Gaining trust, 268-74
Grabbing attention, 117-18
Identification, 7-10
Identification exercise, 7-8
Language, 268-74, 278
Multiple, 14
Unknown, 13-14

Recency, 276
Redundant phrases, 107-110
Exercises, 107-108, 109-110
Repeats, 140, 142-43
Repetition and rhythm, 277-78
Response 198, 203, 248, 265, 269, 271, 273
Rest, 31-32
Résumés, 187-92
Exercises, 189-90, 191-92
Rhythm, 277-78
Rules vs. opinion, 84-85

S

Sabin, William, 304
Salutation, 181-182, 193, 197

Semicolon, 49, 50
Sentence
    Complete, 44, 48, 181
    Complex, 249, 252
    Conversational, 254
    Formal, 250, 252, 256
    Format, 162
    Incomplete, 187, 190, 192
    Length, 121, 162, 171
Sentence (*continued*)
    Misaligned, 116
    Simple, 249, 254, 256
    Transition, 158
    Variety, 94, 121, 162, 167-71
Series separator and commas, 45
Shape, 140, 144-45
Signature line – *See Closing, Email Message Opening and Closing*
Simple words, 100
Spacing, 235
Spell checker, 54, 71, 93
Status reports, 211-20
    Exercises, 215-18, 219-20
Stick people, 9-10
Stories
    Correctness, 38
    Effectiveness, 96
    Finesse, 246
    Style and Format, 174
    Up-front thinking, 2
    Vanity, 134
Strategies for persuasion, 275
Strunk, William, 304
Style Guide, 193
Style, 234, 248-54, 256, 283-84
    Exercises, 251-52, 253-54
    Position Guidelines, 249
    Purpose Guidelines, 250
Style, 303

Subject, 5, 13, 116-17, 176

T

Tact – *See Diplomacy*
Take the Bully by the Horns, 265, 304
The Elements of Style, 304
Thompson, George, 265, 304
Title, job 8
Title, 149, 157, 231, 250, 252, 254
Tone, 176, 248, 292
Topic, 5, 6, 7, 12, 19, 20, 22, 23, 34-35, 173, 176, 180, 200, 202, 208
Transitions, 158
Trim, 140-43
Trip Report, 213
    Exercise, 219-20

U

Unnecessary words, 103-106
    Exercises, 103-104, 105-106
Up-front thinking
    Benefits of, 1, 3, 13
    Brainstorming, 12
    Exercise, 4
    Purpose for writing, 5
    Reader identification, 7-10
    Story, 2
Usage, 85

V

Vanity, 133-36
    Exercise, 135-36
    Story, 134
Variety, 162-66
    Exercises, 163-64, 165-66
Verbal Judo, 265, 304
Verbs
    Abstractions, 118
    Action verbs, 117-118

Announcements, 118
Bureaucratic, 111
Buried verbs, 100
Conflicted, 113
Matching plurals and singulars, 56-60, 89
   Simple vs. complex verbs, 117
   Tense, 89
   Unneeded verbs, 118

W

White, Elwyn, 304
Who vs. Whom, 68-70, 82
   Exercise, 69-70
Williams, Joseph, 303
Wind response to heated email, 258-60, 266
   Exercise, 263-64
Wordiness, 100-102
   Exercise, 101-102
Words That Change Minds, 303
Writing
   Making it easier, 14, 66
   To superiors, 248-250
Writing for Results, 81, 304

Y

Young, James Webb, 32
Yudkin, Marcia, 303

List of Exercises

Active/passive voice, 153-54

Announcements, 177-78, 179-80

Apostrophes, 41-42

Bias, 129-30

BrBrBp Roadmap, 288-91

Bureaucratic verbs, 111-12

ChAMP Interview, 288-91

Commas, 45-46

Compelling edits, 288-91

Conflicted verbs, 113-14, 115

Creativity, 31

Diplomat and director (ordering), 22-23

Drivel, 132

Earth response to heated email, 261-62

Email subject line, 203-204

Flow, 159-60

Formatting, 237-38

Gaining reader's trust, 271-72, 273-74

Homonyms, 73-74

Hooks, 157

Idioms, 75-76, 77-78, 79-80

Impact, 147-148

Layout, 240-42

Matching modifiers, 63-64

Matching pronouns, 61-62

Matching verbs, 57-60
Negativity, 125-26
Numbers, 225-26
Opening line, 17-18
Outlining, 25-28
Parallels, 155-56
Progress report, 215-18
Proofreading, 91-92
Punctuation, 51-52
Pyramid logic for reports, 209-210
Reader identification and analysis, 7-8
Reader visualization, 9-10
Résumés, 189-90, 191-92
Rules, usage and opinions, 85-86
Sentence variety, 163-64, 165-66
Style: Position and Purpose, 251-52, 253-54
Subject and purpose for writing, 5-6
Trip Report, 215-20
Unnecessary verbs, 119-20
Unnecessary words, 103-104, 105-106
Up-front thinking, 4
Vanity, 135-36
Who vs. whom, 69-70
Wind response to heated email, 262-64
Wordiness, 101-102

Resources

No textbook on writing stands alone. All people who try to help others write better draw on the ideas and advice of the many educators and authors who came before. This book is no exception. Here I list the best parts of my library on this topic.

Style: Ten Lessons in Clarity and Grace, by Joseph Williams, a 309-page paperback published by Addison Wesley Longman in 2000. This book inspired the sections on clear writing and concise writing. If you want to learn more about these topics, this is the book to get. It's a serious textbook used in college courses and even graduate schools. Be ready to work!

Words That Change Minds: Mastering the Language of Influence, by Shelle Charvet, a 221-page paperback published by Kendall Hunt in 2001. This book inspired the section on persuasive writing. If you are a student of psychology and want to learn more about applying Neuro-Linguistic Programming to your writing at work, this book is a good place to start.

Persuading on Paper: The Complete Guide to Writing Copy That Pulls in Business, by Marcia Yudkin, a 326-page paperback published by Infinity Publishing in 2001. Nuggets of wisdom in this book inspired the section on promotional writing. It's chock full of tips for anyone preparing marketing materials.

Send: The Essential Guide to Email for Office and Home, by David Shipley and Will Schwalbe, a 245-page hardcover published by Alfred Knopf in 2007. The title says it all. And it's a fun read.

Verbal Judo: The Gentle Art of Persuasion, by George Thompson and Jerry Jenkins, a 222-page paperback published by William Morrow in 1993. This book inspired the concept "be the Wind." It's written by a cop who learned to use words instead of force.

Take the Bully by the Horns: Stop Unethical, Uncooperative, or Unpleasant People from Running and Ruining Your Life, by Sam Horn, a 302-page hardcover published by St. Martin's Press in 2002. This book inspired the concept "be the Earth." To be honest, I hope you never need this book.

The Gregg Reference Manual, by William Sabin, a 610-page spiral-bound reference published by Glencoe McGraw-Hill in 2001. It's not just for administrative assistants. It's for you, no matter who you are. There is no better writing reference to have in your cubicle. Be smart; spend the money.

The Elements of Style, by William Strunk and Elwyn White, a 92-page paperback published by Allyn & Bacon in 1995. I re- read this one every few years to re-learn how to weed my verbiage.

Writing for Results: in Business, Government, and the Professions, by David Ewing, a 448-page hardcover published by John Wiley in 1974. An oldie but a goodie. If you find this red hardback in a used bookstore, snap it up and read it.

Clear Technical Writing, by John Brogan, a 213-page paperback published by Career Education in 1973. The workbook that started it all for me. I scribbled all through it and learned a lot.

Essential English Grammar, by Philip Gucker, a 177-page paperback published by Dover in 1966. A detailed workbook.

www.ingramcontent.com/pod-product-compliance
Lightning Source LLC
Chambersburg PA
CBHW071649090426
42738CB00009B/1472